"Jody tackles a difficult subject with both candor and humor. *All Work & No Say* not only explores the problems that plague the workplace, but also offers positive and sound solutions. This is a book that offers creative ideas and the potential for real change."

Greg Thomas, Editor—weLEAD Online Leadership Magazine
www.leadingtoday.org

All Work

&No SAY

...ho hum another day

**How to Captivate Your Workforce,
Boost Morale and Increase Productivity**

by Jody Urquhart

SECOND EDITION

National Library of Canada Cataloguing in Publication Data

Urquhart, Jody, 1972–
 All Work & No Say—ho hum another day: How to Captivate Your
Workforce, Boost Morale and Increase Productivity / Jody Urquhart.

Includes bibliographical references and index.
ISBN 0-9732502-0-8

1. Management—Employee participation. 2. Communication in business.
3. Industrial relations. I. Title.

HD5650.U76 2003   331'.01'12   C2003-910461-3

Cover and Book Design by Sue Gottschick
basic elements design

Editing by Carol Clarke
Grammar Sharp

Printed in Canada

Thank you to my partner Bill Clennan—the Dean
of Canadian Speakers—for always believing in me.
Without your inspiration the world would be a different place.

Table of Contents

CHAPTER ELEVEN—DEALING WITH CRANKY CO-WORKERS AND CLIENTS
How to Banish Negativity to Keep the Joy of Work Alive 151

Introduction

If you are in a position of management, or if you want to be in a position of management, this book was written for you. It illustrates a belief that employees need involvement and input into their work to be motivated and productive.

Do you remember that old adage, "All work and no play makes Jack a dull boy"? Well, the word is out—all work and no **say** will *also* make Jack a dull boy—not just Jack, but Mary, John, Margaret and your entire workforce. When employees don't have a "say" in their work and its outcome, they put in just another ho-hum day. Without any say in day-to-day decisions, they feel taxed by continually having to go the extra mile in order to feel pride and passion for their efforts. Ultimately, when morale is damaged, it affects the liveliness and inherent joy of work. Working in a place that discounts individual opinions and feeling drains creativity. Slowly, valuable people disengage.

Business As Usual

You've seen it before, probably even experienced it. Employees drag themselves into work half-awake and half-wishing they were somewhere else, dreaming of Friday afternoon. They grieve over their impending work schedules. Sadly, and ironically, professionals insist that their work is satisfying and even fun, but maintain it's the *job* that's the problem. They blame management, work schedules, policy and procedure overkill, a lack of recognition, the feeling of being monitored constantly, or a lack of trust. The joy-devouring list goes on. As a result many employees end up putting in the minimum amount of effort and enthusiasm and the job becomes unrewarding.

One surefire approach to judging the human factor in your workplace is to ask yourself how much **say** employees have in what happens during office hours. Can individual employees make decisions about the outcome of situations, problems and opportunities that arise, or do they have to refer to the policy book to determine the proper course of action?

All Work & No Say will show managers, executives and decision makers how to humanize the workplace, so it's not merely "business as usual." You can transform your workplace by engaging, inspiring and involving employees in fun and productive work. *All Work & No Say* will help remove the barriers that erode passion in your organization.

All Work & No Say is for all organizations that have sidestepped the notion of an engaged and fulfilled workforce. It was not written for the organization that expects its employees to check their hearts at the door and quietly hide behind a smokescreen of detachment. This book is for any conscientious manager who is on a quest to create satisfaction in the workplace.

Chapter One

SAY, SAY, SAY
Captivate Your Workforce!

- Defining an Engaging Workplace
- Measuring Your Organization's Say Factor
- Barriers to the Passionate Workplace
- The Commitment Conundrum
- How to Motivate Indifferent and Complacent Employees
- The Ten Critical Factors to Captivate Your Workforce

What Manage "Meant"

While management may be appointed, leadership has to be earned. Employees promoted to management are often technically very good at the job; they are often strongly independent and task oriented. Yet these qualities don't necessarily make them great leaders. Because they work well alone, they aren't used to involving others—they are prone to being reactive to situations rather than being proactive and *involving* their team.

Managing others requires a bountiful set of skills. Good managers are supportive, helpful, empowering, visionary, accountable, appreciative, able to adapt to change, and good at delegating and prioritizing, among other qualities. All of these leadership traits require that managers learn to free employees' potential for creative expression by *involving* them.

WHAT KIND OF MANAGER ARE YOU?

The Structured Manager: Do you...

Give a lot of directives?
Make most of the decisions?
Condition employees to wait for direction?
Find yourself consumed by problems?
Believe you are very task oriented?

The Involving Manager: Do you...

Involve and ask employees for their help?
Allow others to make decisions about things
    that directly affect them?
Focus on a vision?
Empower others to produce results?
Treat mistakes as opportunities to learn?

Would your people rate you as a Structured or Involving Manager?

The ideas and concepts in this book will help managers move towards being more involving in order to support and empower their workforce.

THREE REASONS WHY JOB INPUT IS ESSENTIAL

Reason #1: Low Job Input =
An Inflexible Workforce
Embracing Change Requires Say

If a business is set up with strong, tight procedures (i.e. do only as the policy book says), allowing little flexibility and input, then it will only do well as long as the circumstances appropriate to those procedures remain unchanged (which is never). Introduce change, and people become a critical factor.

When their jobs require response to changing circumstances, employees must be already well acquainted with thinking creatively and practiced in making quick decisions. Change shouldn't happen *to* employees; it should happen with them. Since they are on the front lines, employees need to feel included in change.

Reason #2: Low Job Input = Low Morale
Do You Love the Job You're With?

Organizations make it hard to "love the job you're with" when they keep denying the strength of input from their employees. They end up with an unmotivated staff that shows up for work thinking, "ho hum another day." A truly successful organization cannot afford to have uninspired, uninvolved employees working solely for a paycheck. A disengaged workforce will contribute a bare minimum effort. In such a work environment, employees make careless and unnecessary mistakes: trust is low; negativity and turnover are high.

Employees will be so busy reacting to what they anticipate their manager wants that their overall effectiveness is diluted.

How can you motivate a workforce when its morale is low? Engage them. Every individual craves whole participation on the job, and that includes their thoughts, feelings and suggestions.

Reason #3: Low Job Input = Low Commitment = High Turnover The Commitment Conundrum

Job turnover represents one of the major expenditures of organizations today. It costs anywhere from $4,000 to $70,000 to hire and train a new employee. *Fortune Magazine's* 2003 report on America's top employers says even though the economy is shifting into low gear, the labor market is still stable, even at companies where a high number of service workers or manual laborers are employed. It is an employees' market, especially for those who are skilled. People find jobs that temporarily fit their needs, and if they don't feel their skills or input are utilized or if they can get paid better elsewhere, they will move. It's a commitment conundrum with employees continually wondering, "Is this job a one-night stand, a quick buck, or is it a life calling?"

It is simply easier to be committed and engaged in an organization that respects your ideas and values your opinion.

JOB INVOLVEMENT IS THE KEY
TO MOTIVATING THE UNMOTIVATED

The Ungrateful Dead

Those who collect their paychecks, but work in a catatonic slumber are true martyrs to their jobs. They are the ungrateful dead. Every organization has them and they are costly. These workplace zombies may not be easy to recognize; they readily hide behind more productive workers. Someone who is doing a below average job doesn't regularly jump up and down to draw personal attention. And you can't really punish someone for being indifferent and detached because the problem may be a personality issue. Consequently, managers often just ignore them. They may discuss the employee behind closed doors with other managers, but rarely confront the offender.

How do we recognize, motivate, or if necessary, terminate these creatures? Give them their say; let them 'fess up to their indifference. If you give employees a chance to explain why they feel the way they do, you can help them sort out the effects of their negative attitudes on performance. Through this process, employees become more accountable. Many apathetic workers maintain the perspective that if a manager doesn't care about them, why should they invest their energy in doing their best? Engaging employees' thoughts, opinions and feelings about their work shows them that you do care.

Studies show that over 70% of communication is non-verbal, so employees pick up on your operative non-verbal cues just as you pick up on theirs. They may think you just don't like them and consequently assume an attitude of indifference towards you. Clear the air by engaging them. Get their input, involve and empower them in key projects that speak to their skills and interests. Create standards and expect employees to be accountable for their own results. Through coaching, you will be able to sort loyalties to know which of the ungrateful dead need to be terminated.

TANGIBLE INTANGIBLES

A Commitment to Intangibles
Will Help Your Organization Grow

Here's the rub: most of the "soft" workplace issues that generate passion and commitment are intangible. Because you can't quantify them, they aren't regarded as scientifically sound. How do you measure the dollar value of a trusted work environment? How do you calibrate the merits of a manager who brings out the best in employees? How do you gauge the worth of an involved and fun workplace? Yet these are the intangible values that will make or break an organization in the twenty-first century.

An organization's best chance to get ahead of its competition is through a commitment to intangibles. Companies that charge a premium justify it through intangibles because not all consumers buy solely on price. Customers are willing to pay more to do business with trusted first class organizations who value their business, treat their employees well, and have sound management principles. Organizations such as Disney, IBM and Starbucks thrive on "soft" issues including customer service, innovation and creativity. In the 1950s, Thomas

Watson Sr. of IBM had an open door policy, whereby any employee could take a complaint to Watson himself. Since workers were assured lifetime employment, they were less afraid to speak their minds. Because its employees felt recognized, IBM became one of America's top employers.

While it is no longer practical to have a lifetime employment guarantee (IBM ditched this policy in the 1990s), it is practical and essential to hear out your employees. Building a fun and engaging workplace requires taking a good look at the intangibles in your organization.

Defining the Say Factor

Simply put, your organization's say factor is based on how much say employees at all levels have in their work and its outcomes. Typically, those in a company with the most say also have the most power or control. Usually they have attained the upper reaches of the firm's hierarchy and have set objectives, procedures and policies. Employees at this level control through rules, information and resources. To increase the say factor in an organization, you systematically "spread out" some of that control to the employees who actually do the job.

MEASURING YOUR ORGANIZATION'S SAY FACTOR

On the chart below, underline the level of say your organization currently has and circle (target!) the level you would like to have.

All Work & No Say			**High Say Factor**
1	2	3	4

LEVELS OF SAY

Level 1: All Work & No Say

- the organization* creates objectives
- the organization tells employees how to implement objectives (with detailed job procedures)
- the organization controls and monitors the results

*Note: the "organization" denotes senior executives in top levels of the hierarchy.

Level 2

- the organization creates objectives
- the organization tells employees how to implement objectives
- employees are responsible for their own results (all managers support and coach staff to reach their goals)

Level 3

- the organization creates objectives
- employees implement objectives
- employees are responsible for their own results

Level 4: A High Say Factor

- employees* create their own objectives
- employees implement their own objectives
- employees are responsible for their own results

*Note: "employees" denotes personnel

The level of **say** appropriate for your organization depends on how much control you feel comfortable giving employees, how well employees perform and how much control employees want in their job. Consider sports as an example: some football teams allow their quarterbacks no **say**—all plays are called and sent in by the coach, whereas some quarterbacks like Joe Montana may call all or the majority of his own plays. Joe wouldn't be nearly as valuable to the team if he couldn't rely on his own judgment in choosing his plays. The level of input a player has in choosing an appropriate play depends mostly on the comfort and skill of the player. No one rule can suggest how much control an individual should have.

Larger organizations tend to find it more difficult to cede control to employees because they have so many employees they rely on. There is a correct mix and balance for every organization. The chapters of this book are designed to help every organization, no matter what their level, find and increase their **say** factor for optimum results.

The Critical Factors

How do we fall into the "business as usual" syndrome? Organizations and their managers, through subtle acts, can sabotage the passion from daily work. We need to focus on the critical factors that sap this passion. It takes more than just listening to people to create a fun and engaging workplace.

TEN CRITICAL FACTORS

To Captivate Your workforce, Boost Morale and Increase Productivity!

1. How to build a rewarding acknowledgment program that candidly recognizes your staff in the act of doing well. The best form of acknowledgment is grounded in the idea that employees work because they are committed and want to work. Work and accomplishment is natural and should be treated as such. *(Chapter 2— Caught in the Act: How to Acknowledge Employees Without Turning Them Off);*

2. How to create a trustworthy work environment. People will not engage in sharing their ideas or take risks in an environment that lacks a bond of trust *(Chapter 3— Creating a Trusting Work Environment);*

3. How to have a customer-centered culture. As the name suggests, compassion breeds passion. Make sure your systems, policies and procedures are compassionate and flexible enough to respond to your employees' and customers' needs *(Chapter 4—Build a Bold Service Mentality with Compassionate Systems);*

4. How to create a fun working environment *(Chapter 5—When Hokey Pokey Is What It's All About)*;

5. How to encourage cooperation over competition because teams are far more powerful than individuals *(Chapter 6—For the Good of the Group)*;

6. How to build a listening culture *(Chapter 7—Lessons in Linguistic Chivalry)* that stands on the shoulders of powerful communication skills;

7. How to stop micromanaging and start delegating to the right people *(Chapter 8—How to Stop Micromanaging and Start Delegating)*;

8. How to manage fierce and fiery emotions that sabotage passion in the workplace *(Chapter 9—Managing the Emotional Workplace)*;

9. How to engage employees in a purposeful and meaningful organizational mission, vision and values *(Chapter 10—Fierce Resolve: How to Engage Employees in Your Organization's Philosophy)*;

10. How crankiness and negativity zaps the fun out of work and what to do about it *(Chapter 11—Dealing with Cranky Co-workers and Clients)*;

All chapters revolve around an organization's commitment to increase the **say** factor and turn business as usual into a fun and engaging workplace.

Passion in Action

Picture a fun and engaging workplace. As a car relies on gasoline to move, the engaging workplace counts on employees to get to where it wants to go. Employee thoughts, feelings and opinions fuel operations. Employees are naturally accountable when their own ideas are being incorporated and they want to see them through. Ideas and solutions are anything but conventional since employees relish the challenge. Employees are willing and able to shift gears easily rather than relying on automatic "transitions." The engaging workplace is one where employees don't need to be told what to do because they know they are trusted enough to solve problems. They are accountable for their actions because there is a sense of pride in individual accomplishment. As well, they are more responsive to the environment and adaptable to the changing needs of their customers because they are accustomed to adapting. Best of all, employees are committed to a company that seeks to bring out their best.

Get Them Talking

The common thread throughout **All Work & No Say** is engaging employee input. Equip the organization for conversations with the key players—your staff. Hear them out and get them talking. Include and involve their input and keep the dialogue going. Sounds simple, right? However, the question isn't as simple as how to get employees talking. The task involves creating an organization that stands by its philosophies, keeps rules to a minimum, candidly recognizes its employees, is sympathetic to the situation and clients, practices responsible emotional management, and is fun and engaging for its employees. Organizations are constantly changing in response to the environment and the needs of their customers. We need to provide the culture and framework to allow for continuous dialogue and for employees to be engaged in their passion.

ACTION PLAN

1. Measure your organization's **say** factor now and decide where you want to be.

2. Deal with complacent and indifferent employees **now** by drawing on their input.

3. Make a commitment to train employees in soft skills.

4. Commit to reading and implementing a chapter of this book per month.

Chapter Two

Caught in the Act

How to Acknowledge People without Turning Them Off

- Find Out if Your Award Program
  Is Doing More Harm Than Good
- Four Keys to a Good Acknowledgment
- Learn How to Create a Personalized Rewards Program
- How to Reward "Soft Skills"
- Fifty-five Ways to Personally Reward Employees

Does acknowledging employees impel them to explore their potential further or is it more of a mindless clacking of cliché expressions? Is your recognition program a superficial ploy encroaching on your staff's need to be candidly recognized? Don't be disheartened because many organizations suffer the same twisted fate. Everybody likes to be appreciated for their efforts, but only if they are rewarded and acknowledged in a way that is genuine. Include employees' **say** in the way you salute their efforts. Most companies have a formal way of acknowledging employees with annual award banquets, top sales awards and certificates. If your award program doesn't invite a thunderous reception, it may be because it is too generic.

COMMON PITFALLS TO AWARD PROGRAMS

There are some major pitfalls to generic award programs:

1. The reward is handed down from management and reinforces imbalances in power.

2. It can be patronizing to receive a small award for a large accomplishment.

3. The accomplishment is often a team effort. It fosters resentment when just one person gets the reward.

4. They cause competition.

5. The reward usually occurs annually or semi-annually, thereby greatly postponing recognition for superior daily performance.

6. Salary raises are nice, but seldom motivate people to consistently achieve on the job.

7. Top performers are often the same people every month. A formal award system may become a program that neglects secondary achievements. How is this helping the rest of your staff? You may be causing resentment.

8. The most common flaw of award programs is that they often reward people for doing work they were supposed to do anyway.

Why are formal award systems so popular then? The main advantage to formal awards is that they are easy to administer. All you need to do is calculate how close (or how far) people get to their goal, find the "top achievers" and acknowledge them with your standard reward. This advantage is also the major disadvantage. Formal awards are a "mass acknowledgment" program. They can be very impersonal and don't take into account the strengths, accomplishments, or efforts of individuals. They don't take into account employees' **say.** Formal award systems recognize one narrow aspect of the job (such as increased revenue, sales or productivity) and those few employees who are good at achieving that goal. By contrast, informal recognition programs focus on spontaneous and personal appreciation of employee efforts.

THE ART OF APPRECIATING OTHERS:

Four Qualities of a Good Acknowledgment

Appreciating others is a brilliant and creative act. Managers need to notice and nurture consistent acts of achievement. Yet many managers don't consider showing appreciation a part of their job description. Other managers realize that acknowledgment is important, but they botch the process. Spouting hollow praise too often will bring discouraging results. There is an art to showing appreciation for others. Employees won't be impressed by trite and generic compliments. Most managers could use a bit of practice with thoughtful acknowledgments. According to B.F. Skinner, a good acknowledgment has four qualities. It is consistently:

1. **Specific:** Talk very specifically about what you saw the person do. General motivational clichés like "good team player" will have a lukewarm effect.

2. **Immediate:** Obviously praising someone for something she did nearly a year ago is a waste of time because the best acknowledgment is immediate. "Catch" someone in the act of doing well and compliment the behavior on the spot.

3. **Personal:** Use the person's name and talk about the qualities they bring to the team.

4. **Spontaneous:** Never script compliments or they won't sound sincere.

I would add to this always link individual performance to the overall good of the group. Here is an example: "Mike, congratulations on how you handled that difficult patient just now. He was nasty and not about to give up, but you sympathized, calmed him down and set him straight." This acknowledgment is specific, immediate, personal, and spontaneous.

Next, link individual performance to the good of the group. "Your taking the time to explain things to that patient builds understanding and agreement and makes that patient so much easier for the rest of the team to deal with."

According to a study done by Robert Half International Limited, a lack of praise and recognition is one of the primary reasons why employees leave their jobs.

Action Plan

Acknowledgment doesn't have to come from a manager. Train and encourage all employees to recognize each other. Train in the four steps above and have employees role-play to acknowledge one another. Create a culture of appreciation (see below) where employees regularly recognize each other's contributions.

Rewards That Increase Say and Engage Employees

Increasing the **say** factor in your organization means increasing employee input to their jobs. Reward people individually and in a personalized way for their accomplishments instead of generally addressing the whole group for its performance level. Take time to find out what specifically motivates each of your employees and then see what you can do to make those things happen. How do you find out what motivates others? Ask them. Increase the **say** factor in the job by getting people talking about what inspires and motivates them and engage them in the reward process. When people get rewarded in the way they want, they will be much more satisfied. Involvement equals commitment. The best management is what you do *with* others, not *to* them.

FOUR STEPS TO CREATING
A PERSONALIZED REWARDS SYSTEM:

1. Create an acknowledgment committee. This is a fun volunteer position and it should rotate regularly so all staff have an opportunity to participate. The acknowledgment committee is responsible for acknowledging other staff members weekly.

2. Have the acknowledgment committee create a form that helps them get to know employees. Ask employees things like, "Share your favorite color, your biggest pet peeve, something interesting about your family, your hobbies…" Anything unique about a person that they would offer to share is valuable.

3. File these forms away and every week (or month or however often) the committee randomly draws an employee's name and checks the list to find interesting unique ways to acknowledge him. (e.g. Jason loves telling jokes so buy him a joke book). The "reward" is fun and does not cost a lot (usually under $10).

4. The committee now has to catch Jason in the act of doing well and acknowledges him with the personalized item. You may even create a fun ritual, chant or saying when delivering acknowledgments.

REWARD THE INTANGIBLE

As a rule, performance evaluations focus on mental functions such as comparing, copying, compiling, analyzing, coordinating and synthesizing information. True, these are important parts of the job, yet they only represent a portion of an employee's contribution. In a recent survey of chief information officers, 85% of respondents said they look for well-developed soft skills, including business acumen and interpersonal abilities when evaluating job candidates. Soft skills, according to 68% of those polled, are more important today than they were just five years ago. The survey was conducted by an independent research firm, which targeted a hundred and fifty executives from a thousand of the nation's largest companies. *(PR Newswire)*.

In an employment interview, typical questions posed are about how well people relate to others, how well they deal with conflict etc. These traits are part of the system of "soft" skills. We hire people for these qualities, yet rarely do organizations reward employees for having or developing them. Why? Soft skills are hard to measure. How well someone deals with conflict, for instance, isn't easy to calculate on a standard scale.

Nonetheless, learn to recognize soft skills: how employees communicate, negotiate, deal with conflict, work with others, handle change, handle stress, and manage others.

You can discover them in conversation. Get employees to talk and solicit their input with questions like:

- That situation must have irritated you. How did you respond?

- How did you resolve that conflict with a co-worker or client?

- If you wrote in our company newsletter and had to describe yourself in only three words, what would those words be? (Develops personal awareness)

- What risks did you take this week? What was it like? What was the result?

- What kinds of tasks do you not enjoy doing? How do you manage to motivate yourself to complete those tasks? (This develops self-motivation.)

We know we can't measure the intangible aspects of the job. That's why it's really important that employees have a clear vision of the goal and how to achieve it. (e.g. "What would showing more initiative look like or feel like?"). Reflection allows employees to examine their progress toward developing pro-active behaviors.

The first step is recognizing their "soft skills" that need to be developed, and the next step is developing them. Have employees come back weekly or monthly and talk about their goals and how and if they met them.

You could also reinforce awards annually for showing initiative, taking risks, contributing to the team and more. Staff would vote for their co-workers in these categories throughout the year. Hand the awards out at a yearly event. Have employees briefly write down why they voted for each person.

Collect those responses weekly and you will have a really good idea of how well people work together. You'll also be getting staff input for helping you "catch" others in the act of doing well. You can use this feedback to acknowledge employees at their next coaching session.

CAUGHT IN THE ACT OF DOING WELL

Once a manager knows the tangible goals and intangible skills individual employees are working towards, and what specifically motivates each individual, now comes the fun part—catching employees in the act of doing well, and acknowledging them with informal rewards.

Once you create an informal reward profile for each employee based on their likes, pet peeves, greatest strengths and more, you can surprise them. Try personal thank you notes, balloon-o-grams, movie passes and more. (See *Fifty-five Ways to Personally Reward Employees* at the end of the chapter for more examples.)

To really increase the impact, make sure the rewards are personal. Be creative to match the reward with personal interests or special needs. If an employee has a son who loves hockey, reward him with tickets to a hockey game. An employee has a daughter who is getting married? Give her a bridal magazine and tickets to a bridal show. An employee has a spouse who has cancer? Give her time off to volunteer for this cause. An employee's son just got his driver's license? Give him a book about handling teenage drivers. An employee who loves to golf? Buy him a round of golf. Use your imagination and the input of fellow employees to choose just the right reward.

A Culture of Appreciation

The best form of acknowledgment is grounded on the idea that people work because they are committed and want to work. This assumes people work for reasons other than a salary at the end of the week or an award at the end of a project. Work and accomplishment are natural companions and should be treated as such. As Alfie Kohn observes in *Punish by Reward:*

"When responsible action, the natural love of learning, and the desire to do good work are already part of who we are, then the tacit assumption to the contrary can be fairly described as dehumanizing."

Consider a company with an attitude of appreciation that is a routine part of every day. Everyone respects and acknowledges each other and you don't have to be a manager to do that. Employees, aware of the specific projects or roles their colleagues are involved in as well as their strengths are on the lookout to catch people doing well. This culture assumes people are out to do their best and regularly observes them doing it. Sincere and genuine appreciation is always forthcoming. Employees are at their best because their standards of excellence are their own.

KEYS TO BETTER PERFORMANCE

How do you create this kind of culture of appreciation?

1. Avoid awards that set people apart from each other, such as programs for the top sales person. Only one person can win this award, so only few will try. It also separates winners from losers.

2. Let employees set their own goals. Show you understand how their energy helps the team and company, and acknowledge their contributions.

3. Encourage employees to acknowledge others daily. Set up an informal network, like a newsletter or bulletin board where people can brag about their colleagues.

4. Give employees the opportunity during meetings to talk about what they accomplished that week. In other words, let them brag about themselves.

5. Recognize people for more than specific projects or achievements. How does each individual's strength contribute to the team as a whole?

6. Make every employee aware of each other's strengths and give them a chance to learn from one another.

7. Continuously recognize the achievements of the group as a whole. Allow them to savor the feeling of achievement.

8. Reinforce the value of the work itself because the caliber of their functions affects their customers.

9. Celebrate the vision of the company and how the group, made up of the individuals within it, helps to achieve that vision.

10. Design incentives to reward departments for the whole group's accomplishments. Create a work environment where people will wish to contribute and succeed. Employees expect to be involved. To help your employees and managers work together towards common goals, include your corporate core values into the program. If your organization boasts customer service, include several aspects of this on the performance evaluation.

MOTIVATING WITHOUT THE CARROT

Motivating people individually means focusing less on a generic reward system and more on candid personalized recognition. Reward people as soon as you notice them doing well. Incorporate soft skills into your evaluation. What we can accomplish has more to do with what we *think* we can do than what we actually *can* do.

Think about this. If you are convinced you can't meet your "impossible quota," what are the chances you will? They're very slim, of course, almost to the point of proving yourself right. Sometimes, the need to accomplish something is a motivation or force helping people believe they can do it. Managers can be that force. In fact, this may be the main role of the manager—to see better in others than they can see in themselves. Show employees the next level of accomplishment and help them believe they can do it. Once an employee reaches a goal, it raises his individual standard of performance.

The Bottom Line

Companies with an attitude of appreciation are proud of the achievements of all employees and departments. They are aware of the strengths of each individual in helping realize the corporate vision and communicating this vision is their strong point. They know that acknowledging people can dramatically change the way people interact with each other and with customers.

FIFTY-FIVE WAYS TO MAKE REWARD PROGRAMS MORE FUN AND EFFECTIVE

1. Give employees "time off" to volunteer for their favorite cause.

2. Appoint an employee to do nothing but acknowledge other staff for the day.

3. Give certificates employees can redeem for a "something of their choice" (a day off, extra coaching, extra lunch break, shift preference).

4. Give employees a day to job shadow any job they choose.

5. Create plaques with funny sayings on them.

6. Create "Service Pride Awards" that specifically acknowledge employees for going the extra mile for the team good.

7. Profile a staff member in an article.

8. Have employees write an article about their accomplishment and how they achieved it, then publish it.

9. Have managers "valet park" employees' cars.

10. Give employees a day to visit another department and report back to their co-workers about the experience.

11. Leave a voicemail saying thank you or send an email. (Thank you, I noticed...)

12. Have managers bake cookies or make pizza or pancakes for staff.

13. Sketch a ladder climbing towards a goal where employee accomplishments push the marker up towards the goal.

14. Hand out ribbons or pins saying, "I helped our team reach our goals."

15. Have a "Treasure Chest," where employees select gifts from items such as coffee mugs, pen sets and movie tickets.

16. Give employees fun things to hand out to other staff.

17. Surprise an employee with their favorite coffee and muffin at a coaching session.

18. Send a "Thank you" bouquet of flowers to an employee's spouse.

19. Give employees the opportunity to brag about their

accomplishments on a brag bulletin board, in a newsletter or during a meeting.

20. Recognize the difficult aspects of the job that the staff deals with all the time.

21. Give a group bonus and empower a team to decide what to do with the money.

22. Stand up for employees verbally in front of other staff or clients.

23. Design a "most creative way to serve a customer" award.

24. Let an employee be the "Manager on Duty" for a couple of hours.

25. Take employees to a stand-up comedy club or hire a stand-up comedian.

26. Have a special "Lunch and Learn" program for staff.

27. Deliver a personal thank you note.

28. Have a special hat or item that someone wears for the day.

29. Give concert tickets or sports tickets.

30. Say "Thank you" the moment they did well.

31. Send a balloon-o-gram to their home.

32. Other employees could make a skit about them.

33. Help out with day care.

34. Massage voucher for a local spa.

35. A favorite candy bar.

36. Time off for a family event.

37. Have an acknowledgment newsletter spotlighting employees doing well.

38. Movie passes or dinner certificates.

39. Dry cleaning vouchers.

40. Ask employees their favorite color and put rewards on their desk in this color (pens, mugs, balloons, etc.).

41. Buy lunch.

42. When someone is caught in the act of doing well, put her name in an annual draw for prizes.

43. Donate money to a charity of the employee's choice in his or her name.

44. Employee appreciation lunches.

45. Personalized memo pads, pens, etc.

46. "I Believe in You" recognition pieces for people struggling toward a more difficult goal over a longer time (e.g. taking night classes towards a degree).

47. Send employees to an industry conference you know they will value.

48. Establish special fun programs for staff to participate in.

49. Create "Leadership Development Awards."

50. Give "Character" awards (Showing Determination, Initiative, Risk Taking).

51. Have a "Keep Your Cool" Award for staying calm during a difficult challenge.

52. Reward employees for doing their jobs, not just keeping them.

53. "Employee Recognition" events with organized sports and games.

54. "Casual Dress" days.

55. Contest fun (e.g. the most creative way to deal with a customer complaint).

ACTION PLAN

1. Assess your current rewards system.

2. Create a personalized reward system.

3. Create an acknowledgment committee.

4. Practice the four steps to a good acknowledgment.

5. Implement several of the 55 ways to make your rewards program more fun.

Other Resources:

Fast Feedback by Bruce Tulgan.

The 8 Best Practices of Exceptional Companies by Jack Fitz-Enz.

Constructive Appraisals by Roy Lecky-Thompson.

Bob Nelson, author of the best-selling *1001 Ways to Reward Employees* (Workman Publishing, 1994) and *1001 Ways to Energize Employees* (Workman Publishing, 1997)

Performance Appraisals by SHRM Information Center.

Chapter Three

Creating a Trusting Work Environment

Seven Steps to Increase Trust in Your Workplace

- Assess the Level of Trust in Your Workplace
- Understand How Trust Affects the Bottom Line
- Seven Steps to Increase Trust in Your Workplace

Imagine a workplace that relies on fraud, deceit and regular scams as a way of doing business. Its niche is carved out of false promises and open lies. Thankfully, most organizations like this only enjoy a very brief existence. Contrast the very corrupt organization with one holding a spotless record and unblemished past, and it becomes logical that many organizations fit somewhere between these two extremes. Tenuous balances of trust underlie all business activity. One factor that will negatively affect your organization's level of **say** is suspicion. If employees don't feel trusted, they will guard their words and be reluctant to offer input. The job becomes ***All Work & No Say*** as soon as a lack of trust steals the passion away.

SYMPHONY OF TRUST

How much do you trust your staff and why does it matter? Trust affects the bottom line: the way you treat your employees is the way they will treat clients. If it's acceptable that an organization or manager doesn't have to keep promises, then you can almost guarantee employees won't be keeping promises to clients either.

"People do business with people they trust." You've heard this before. A client's trust in an organization starts with an organization's trust in its employees. As Lance Secretan quips in *Reclaiming Higher Ground*, "Our society is suffering from truth decay." He holds that, especially in teams, telling the truth is essential to good business. "If the members of a symphony lie to each other, they will play awful music," he maintains. So it goes in any team environment. Another compelling advantage for telling the truth is that it's efficient. Over a third of an organization's budget may be devoted to administrative functions such as controls, reports and procedures. Many controls exist because management doesn't trust employees. What if we could nix some of these controls and trust each other to do our best? It would be much less expensive and much more efficient.

EXPLODING THE TRUST MYTH: "WE TRUST EACH OTHER"

Many organizations think that trust isn't a concern. On the surface everything is fine, but on closer inspection one might discover that employees are seeking to satisfy only their basic immediate needs. Their passion is lost in the details of the job.

Over time, working in such an atmosphere precipitates lethargy for some, and for others, illness.

Advantages to an Open Trusting Workplace

- Employees are more willing to contribute their ideas.

- Saves resources (time and money).

- Fuels creativity, innovation and productivity.

- Encourages controlled risk taking.

- "Forbidden topics" create fear and take up a lot of personal energy that can be freed up and used for more productive work.

- Employees will be more eager to get involved knowing they are trusted. More involved = more motivated.

- Promotes richer relationships among staff.

A TEST: IS LOW TRUST AFFECTING YOUR ORGANIZATION?

Here are some things companies do that cripple the trust factor. Answer **yes** or **no** to the questions below to test your trust factor:

1. Do managers in your organization forget to model what they say? (e.g.: An organization says the most important asset is its people, but then they make changes that affect all employees without notice or input.)

   ☐ YES   ☐ NO

American aviation pioneer Wilbur Wright said, *"A parrot talks much but flies little."*

2. Do managers make promises they can't keep? (e.g.: Managers keep talking about a better, fairer scheduling system that never materializes.)

   ☐ YES ☐ NO

3. Do managers tend to avoid dealing with conflict? This comes across in a false persona: "Everything is just great!"

   ☐ YES ☐ NO

4. Does your organization guard and selectively disclose information? (e.g.: There are off-limit zones for some employees. Information is guarded and only a select few are in the know. Meetings happen behind closed doors.)

   ☐ YES ☐ NO

5. Does your organization discourage employees from using their own judgment? (e.g.: The organization always goes by the book. There are several rules designed so that people don't have to think about what they should do.)

   ☐ YES ☐ NO

6. Do managers ask for input and suggestions, then ignore them? (e.g.: A manager asks for suggestions on improving service. An employee offers two good ideas and no one says anything or brings it up again. Employees get the feeling that management is just going through the motions, and they really don't want the input.)

☐ YES   ☐ NO

Note: Of course, you won't use all ideas, but follow-up is essential. It shows you are listening.

7. Does it seem like everything is monitored, from the number of sick days to productivity levels?

☐ YES   ☐ NO

8. Are employees "given" information (change in job, new policies and procedures) and not included in it?

☐ YES   ☐ NO

Note: Quality information that is formally and consistently shared builds trust. It softens the barriers between "us" and "them" thinking.

9. Does your organization encourage competition among its members?

☐ YES   ☐ NO

Note: In a competitive workplace employees will not share information to help one another succeed. Competition reinforces the notion that the end justifies the means.

SCORE: If you answered **yes** to **three** or more of the questions above, then trust is likely affecting morale in your workplace.

DEFINING A TRUSTING WORKPLACE

When I speak to organizations about creating trust in the workplace, these are the most common observations participants shared about trustworthy companies and individuals:

"She has never let me down."

"They do what they say they will do."

"I know the organization has my best interests in mind."

"He knows what he's talking about and admits it when he doesn't."

HOW TO BUILD TRUST THROUGH INFORMATION

Imagine your first day on the job in a new organization. As you walk in the door, you notice rooms that are off-limits to everyone but the manager. Day after day, you see that information is carefully guarded and watched. Meetings occur behind closed doors. As managers walk around, you sense they know something you don't. Does this sound like a fun and productive work environment?

What's the big deal? Why do we guard information so carefully? Company information is often seen as intellectual property for both the organization and for individuals who develop it. People put effort into creating information and ideas and start to take ownership of them. In doing so, it becomes territorial and guarded. Pretty soon, a wedge develops between those who have access to information and those who don't. Individuals start to see they are excluded and feel disconnected from the whole vision of the organization. This diminishes trust and it causes people to guard their ideas and limit their input.

Information bonds people to one another. It is an important part of the positive growth and sense of community within an organization. Cutting people off from access to information is unhealthy for progress. Find ways to make information accessible to everyone. If meetings must occur behind closed doors, make sure others in the department are included. Encourage them to bring their information and ideas to the meeting. Create an after meeting follow-up bulletin that discusses what was said. Much of the important information you get will not be written. Instead, it comes in chance conversations, briefly mentioned in meetings, in the elevator or in the lunchroom. Verify important information and make a point of distributing it to employees.

Explain the reason for any change, and how it will serve management, employees, customers, suppliers, etc. Keep employees well informed of what is going on, why it is happening, and how it affects their job and the organization as a whole. Ask for suggestions and involve everyone as much as possible. Remember that employees are the resource that makes things happen; therefore, it is essential to get their buy-in.

Managing information may be tricky. While you want to keep people informed, you don't want to overwhelm them with information they don't need to know. Presentation is the key. Here is a method to handle information:

A COMMUNICATION SYSTEM TO MAKE INFORMATION ACCESSIBLE AND BUILD TRUST

Decide on the type of information and how you should disseminate it:

1. **Organizational philosophy** is anything related to the long-term mission, vision or direction of the organization. This information is very relevant to all employees because it is the "glue" that holds diverse departments of an organization together in a shared purpose. However, it does not need to be presented at year-end when everyone is swamped with work. Save this information and present the bigger picture on a monthly basis to help staff maintain focus. You may also have a newsletter devoted to initiatives that support the organization's purpose and vision.

2. **Operations and procedures**. If information relates directly to an employee's day-to-day job, the sooner she

knows about it the better. If information is important, you need a consistent system to disseminate it efficiently and effectively. That may be through staff meetings, individual coaching, bulletins or announcements. If the information is critical to the job, then a feedback or follow-up procedure will be necessary to ensure it is being incorporated. Develop a channel strictly for sharing critical information so that employees pay attention.

3. **Incomplete information**. Very often managers will hear word of potentially "nasty" things like mergers or layoffs that would affect staff adversely. Some of this information may be sensitive and still tentative. If you don't have full information, you run the risk of putting people on the defensive. Since they don't have all the pieces of the complete puzzle they may rush to false conclusions which puts you in an awkward situation. Information should be communicated in a uniform and consistent way to prevent a "leak" of partial facts, which will be subject to rumor and false conclusions. Beware of selectively putting some people in the know and not others.

If you consistently organize and disseminate information through established means, then it is more readily understood. Employees will get used to getting updates about directives once a month in a meeting and will develop ways to utilize the information.

Make Mistakes More Often

Encourage employees to risk making mistakes and create an atmosphere that encourages them to be open when errors occur. When people make mistakes they usually feel guilty and try to cover up—an unfortunate reaction that inhibits the learning process. Mistakes are a part of growth. Permit them to be shared so that others may also learn from the example. This will foster an environment of openness that encourages creativity and autonomy. Celebrate solving mistakes as a victory.

Communicate: Why and How

Strategic changes in an organization are usually created by higher-level executives and are initiated for a very good reason. Change supports the organization's mission, vision, and values, but by the time change reaches your department and affects your clients and staff it's usually presented as *tactics.* In other words, we are very good at explaining how change will occur and how it will affect our jobs, but we forget to explain why. The "why" embodies the purpose and the meaning of any new activity. Once employees understand "why", the "how" often falls into more readily into place. Open the lines of communication. Employees should feel comfortable talking openly and informally in a setting where everyone's opinion is given equal consideration. When change occurs, employees should be included and involved.

SEVEN STEPS TO BUILDING A TRUSTING WORKPLACE:

Step 1—Dialogue: Most importantly, focus on opening the lines of communication. Get people talking and make it a safe atmosphere for employees to share their honest opinions. Discuss the importance of open communication with all leaders.

Step 2—Acknowledge the Unspeakable: Do people hate the overtime policy? Do you have low morale at the office? Are several managers abusing privileges? Touchy issues need to be resolved and openly discussed. Many employees will be quietly harboring ill feelings about such "unspeakables." It is essential to open the lines of communication. Be careful not to point fingers or place blame inappropriately. Stick to the facts: what's been happening, why, and what you intend to do about it.

Step 3—Secrecy Breeds Suspicion: When information or activity is kept secret, it is open to misinterpretation, so communication is essential. Develop tools that help communicate what's going on. Regular email, meetings, newsletters, conference calls, or voicemail keep people in the know. Any new discussion or planning should be shared with all employees sooner than later. Activate your communication system to make information accessible.

Step 4—Keep Promises: Make fewer and better agreements. Don't commit to something that you can't follow through with. If you can't honor an undertaking or proposal, then say so right away and renegotiate. Keep people in the know (e.g.: we are not going to be able to... and here's why…). Express your regrets and talk about what you plan to do about the problem. Communicate that everyone should be accountable; every level of staff should keep promises. Involve the whole group and advocate everyone's accountability. Invest in commitments.

Step 5—Eliminate Ambiguous Behavior: Anything that isn't necessary, or that you can't justify, eliminate. There should be a sound purpose for all activities.

Step 6—Managers Need to Model Trust: Is management consistent, predictable, and trustworthy? All managers should be evaluated along with staff.

Step 7—Rules Should Be Treated as Guidelines, Not Solutions: Employee judgment should be valued to create trusting relationships.

Involve, Involve, Involve. If employees come to you with a concern, why not involve them in the solution? Let them gather a task force and come up with several possible solutions to present to management and other staff. The more involved the naysayers are, the more the problem becomes their own and they take responsibility for it (and the way they feel).

Implement each of the above seven steps in phases. The creation of an open trusting work environment that involves and includes employee input means that all feelings need to be heard, including criticism. Management must be prepared to welcome and handle employee criticism.

HOW TO ENCOURAGE CRITICISM
WITHOUT LOSING CONTROL

This may seem challenging, but the idea is to create an open workspace where it is safe to support one another. How can you accomplish this if employees are afraid to tell managers how they feel? We are not talking outright warfare or blame but ways to establish discussing criticism with managers. Encourage input at individual coaching sessions by asking "Is there anything that has been bothering you that you would like to talk about?" Hold forums where employees can anonymously "get it off their chests" by offering feedback to a manager's weekly review box. Make sure employees realize that not every criticism can be addressed, especially if it's anonymous. To prepare employees for using a "feedback box," stress the need for a positive tone and helpful remedies. Anonymous criticism can be acknowledged in a quarterly "Critique" newsletter. This could be a "Talk to Management" column. The employee addresses the complaint. The newsletter publishes the (anonymous) letter and managers respond to it. Encourage input in a regular "Let's Talk" focus group where employees are invited to vent about anything they want with their co-workers.

A key challenge for management is responding to criticism of policies or procedures that affect employees but cannot be changed. It is important to handle these critiques in a straightforward and direct manner.

How to Respond to Criticism of Organizational Policies That Can't Be Changed

1. Express empathy and understanding. "We know these reports can be very frustrating as they take up a lot of your time and don't yield direct results."

2. Provide reasons (the "why") for the offending regulation. "We really rely on these reports being filled out accurately because they help us keep track of what is going on in the fields. Without them we would..."

3. Explain any actions the management will do to address the complaint.

4. Close the response on a positive note.

Too Scared to Trust? Fear Is a Natural Reaction

I'm not suggesting abandoning all rules, throwing management to the wind, or letting people have free reign in their jobs.

Ask employees about their comfort levels. Look at an individual's capabilities and history. You wouldn't ask someone excessively shy, with few communication skills, to do a speech for your shareholders. Adding trust and responsibility to a job takes small steps, not huge leaps. This helps employees to predict the behavior of others and minimizes the risk associated with counting on them. Too often plans are not successfully implemented because the appropriate culture is not in place. Strategies are created behind closed doors and given to staff to execute. Like a deer caught in the glare of headlights, employees are stunned by new roles that come speeding towards them. They may not feel comfortable, prepared or confident in the newly appointed role. Allow them to express possible misgivings about the task and to prepare themselves before implementing it.

Final Say

Who gets the final **say**? Your employees do. Build trust in your office by involving employees and including their input. Engage them as part of the problem and they will surprise you with honest solutions. The foundation of trust in any organization is built on a concrete base of openness and input from others.

ACTION PLAN

1. Assess the level of trust in your workplace.

2. Evaluate your communication system and make information more accessible.

3. Complete and gradually implement the seven steps to increase trust in your workplace.

Chapter Four

Build a Bold Service Mentality with Compassionate Systems

What to Do When Your Systems Speak Louder Than Your People

- The Compassionate System and How It Affects Service
- The Pitfalls of Rules
- Four Steps to Create Compassionate Service Systems
- When to Create Rules
- How to Create a **Bold** Service Mentality
- Two Essential Steps to Cement Your Bold Service Mentality

WHAT IS A COMPASSIONATE SYSTEM?

A bold customer service mentality requires compassionate systems. What is a compassionate system? Systems are usually created from processes as a way to organize people or information. To make sure objectives are accomplished, organizations "systemize" the process. Out of systems come rules, policies and controls. A compassionate system is one that is flexible enough to respond to the needs of the situation and everyone involved (both staff and customer). Compassionate systems create an environment where employees are empowered to use their judgment to make decisions (thereby responding to customers instead of reacting with set policies or procedures). The reasoning is much like General George S. Patton's belief in giving bright people direction and letting them figure out the details of how to accomplish the goal. A compassionate system allows people to be in control of their environment and provide **bold service**.

Training for this kind of service isn't just a one-shot experience. It is a mentality that starts with the organization as a whole. Because people provide service, this usually means empowering employees to make more decisions, define service in their own terms and take ownership of their own service standards.

LOUD SYSTEMS DISCOURAGE INPUT AND DESTROY SERVICE

A loud and rigid system is an inflexible one. It puts policies before people. The rules are clear and binding and there are no exceptions. Employees in these organizations learn their input isn't valued. They learn not to think on their feet or take initiative to help others. Both employees and clients who deal with these organizations learn to take no for a consistent answer.

Not My Job Description

Roles and responsibilities in an organization are often conveniently broken down from person to person. It makes sense from a business perspective, but it can be unfortunate and time consuming for a client. Employees are trained to do their jobs and anything that falls outside their jurisdiction gets passed along to someone else. Customers dealing with an employee in an organization with inflexible systems are met with empty answers and blank looks if they speak to the wrong individual. They are sent hunting for the person who is "in charge" to take care of them.

The easiest way to create a compassionate system is to tackle it situation by situation. You'll need to challenge the existing rules.

RULES THAT BLIND: THE PITFALLS OF RULES

Organizations with inflexible systems have rules for everything from holidays to bathroom breaks. Does your organization have a policy for when it's appropriate to create a rule? Most don't; instead, they create one whenever an issue comes up that affects operations. This approach is based on the fear that things can and will go wrong.

Too many rules render you helplessly spending all your time enforcing them. Some people argue that rules add structure. A certain amount of structure creates freedom because guidelines liberate people and make them more productive. However, most organizations place too much emphasis on structure and not enough on their people. Rules can create inflexible systems. Below are some of the pitfalls of rules:

1. They create inflexible uncompassionate systems. Applying the same rules to everyone can cause resentment. Different people have special circumstances. If these are ignored, people feel ignored.

2. Too many rules create an atmosphere of prohibition.

Employees learn not to rely on their own judgment. Instead of becoming quick thinkers and taking risks, they use the rules as their fall back position.

3. If it's not in the rulebook, employees may not do it.

4. Relying on static rules deprives employees of their creativity.

5. Rules give rise to more rules, which cause a lot of administration and, in the long run, are very costly.

6. Usually, rules spill onto customers. Soon, if potential clients want to buy from your company, they must first study and abide by the terms. They could just go somewhere else.

7. Too many rules communicate a lack of trust in employees.

8. Rules create an attitude. Employees mimic this attitude and it affects how they deal with suppliers and customers. For example, if the company has a strict policy about payment terms, employees are expected to remind clients about those terms through telephone calls or repeated mailings. Even though they are just doing their jobs, the personnel are forced to annoy customers.

9. Rules affect the atmosphere for both employees and customers. Everyone has had the experience of walking into a store to be greeted with signs like "Do not touch!" or "You break it—you pay." Imagine being invited into someone's home and seeing signs like these. Would you be eager to come back?

10. Managers become parole officers enforcing rules. They get so caught up in who did what wrong, they forget to lead and end up babysitting.

How Rules Are Set

How are rules set? One of the more popular methods works this way: an employee may do something undesirable, so management creates a policy that punishes everyone. Actually, rules may be set this way in every facet of the organization. Consider this example: a few customer checks bounce, so the organization sets a policy to accept no personal checks. It's hard to estimate how much lost business is directly related to this new policy.

Rules are also set strategically. An organization has objectives and it creates rules to make sure things happen. Instead, why not concentrate on empowering employees to achieve goals rather than punishing them with more rules?

Power Comes from People

Effective managers know power comes from people. The manager's role is not to have ultimate control by enforcing rules, but to support and coordinate employees' efforts. This may be a complete attitude shift for some managers who are used to being in charge.

In most organizations, managers are also expected to be leaders. They can most effectively lead by empowering employees to use their own judgment and skills to benefit the organization. Can you trust people to do their jobs without all the rules and controls? Yes. Most people do the right thing when left to their own judgment. If you tell employees what to do, they will automatically do it your way without calling on their own creativity and judgment. After a while, this creates a stale work environment. Instead of being alive with creative ideas flowing, people dutifully do their jobs.

Empower Employees to Rely on Their Judgment

How do you stop relying on rules to create more compassionate systems? Empower employees to solve problems on their own, making them a part of the solution. Get them asking, "What is the best way to handle this?" Then, provide them with the resources and support to do it. For example, let's say it is taking employees too long to go through their email every day. Instead of creating a policy that limits the time spent picking up email, ask employees, "How can we use our email system more effectively?" Let employees come up with the solution. Being a part of the solution makes employees more accountable, creating much less paperwork and formality.

For larger organizations it's more difficult to have compassionate systems and put the power into staff. It takes a tremendous amount of trust, so start slowly.

FIVE STEPS TO CREATING
COMPASSIONATE SERVICE SYSTEMS

1. Do you currently have policies that do not serve customers or staff? These likely serve the organization as a whole, but do they affect the relationship between frontline service people and clients? Re-examine them asking, "How does this policy help our employees do their jobs or our clients get what they want?" Does it help you build a positive, helpful service outlook? If not, consider why you have it in the first place and whether the policy should be changed or made more flexible based on the situation.

2. Go through different work scenarios and ask, "Can we substitute individual judgment for the rules in this situation?"

3. Gradually encourage competent employees you trust to rely on their judgment and solve problems on their own.

4. Even if employees can't be involved in creating policies and procedures, let them be a part of their implementation. For example, a new policy is to have all accounts receivable collected within 30 days. Involve employees in the implementation (How can we collect those accounts more quickly?). Employees will be the best judges of the answers since they are aware of clients with special circumstances who will require unique approaches.

5. Finally, always make sure that employees know the reasons behind policies, rules and systems; they need to understand the rationale to better implement them. Often rules get in the way of helping a customer, and employees need to be prepared to explain and justify them.

The level of accountability appropriate for your organization depends on how much control you feel comfortable giving employees. There is a right mix and balance for every organization.

KNOW WHEN TO CREATE RULES

Decide how and when you will set rules. Instead of setting them on the spot whenever it seems necessary, decide in advance what is appropriate. For example, rules are often necessary for routine performance to prevent chaos. If someone comes to you requiring the development of a rule, ask:

- How many people does this directly affect?

- Will this rule help us deal with future situations or is it just creating more paperwork?

- Is this something that we can empower employees to use their own judgment to deal with (in which case you may not need the rule)?

- How can I involve all people who are affected by this policy?

HOW TO REINFORCE A BOLD SERVICE MENTALITY

A service mentality begins with the combination of a compassionate system and a **bold** service vision. A vision is a description of the future that produces passion and is worded in a clear and inspiring way. It should describe the key market you are in, the basic service you provide, the feeling it provokes and what distinguishes you from your competition. Most importantly, it should have meaning for clients and employees. There is no use having a vision if employees don't know what it is or how it affects their job. I suggest regularly reinforcing your vision of service to keep it alive. Do this by reminding people how their jobs keep the spirit and pride of service going and help the organization meet its commitment to clients.

The most important part of the vision is the feeling it evokes. Find examples of areas where this feeling comes through in service and celebrate them. Reinforce that feeling with regular meetings, newsletters and other communications celebrating what your organization is doing and why. Remind employees how their specific job contributes to the organization, the client and the community. People tend to appreciate their work more when they see how much they are contributing to others.

Exercise: Service should be at the core of everything. Your vision reminds people of the reason they are doing what they do. If it is central to the business, it will inspire people. How would employees respond if someone asked, "What does your organization do?" Would they respond, "We produce _____"? If service is at the heart of your business, it should come through loudly and clearly. "We help our customers be more successful by _____."

Have every service employee answer this question in his or her own way and from their answers assess whether a bold service mentality exists.

Two Essential Steps to Cement Your Bold Service Mentality

Step One: Create a culture of *yes*. This doesn't mean you have to agree with everything others say, but you can just change the way you express yourself. This applies to managers speaking to staff and staff speaking to customers. Listen to the difference:

Instead of saying, "I can't give you a raise because you haven't completed all phases of the learning requirements," **say**, "I would be pleased to give you a raise once you complete all phases of the learning requirements."

In both of the examples above you communicate the same thing (you have to complete all phases of the learning before receiving a promotion), but the second one creates an attitude of **yes** and leaves the person more positive and motivated.

This approach applies in the service areas as well. Here is an example: **Instead of saying**, "No, Mr. Jones, I can't change your medication schedule until our next shift schedule is created," **say**, "Mr. Jones, I understand you want to change your medication schedule and I would be happy to do that once our next shift schedule is created."

In the second example you are showing Mr. Jones respect for his request and communicating a positive yes attitude.

Exercise: Create a bold service mentality with a yes attitude. Have both managers and employees role-play and practice re-wording potentially negative responses with a yes attitude. Start the exercise with a list of "no's" that regularly get communicated to customers or clients and brainstorm ways to rephrase them with a positive yes attitude.

Step Two: Empower employees. We have all had the frustrating experience of having to tell a customer that as much as we would like to help, we cannot because the system is inflexible, and we don't have the authority. I was the convention co-chair for the *2002 Simply World Class Convention* for the Canadian Association of Professional Speakers. We hosted this event at the Sheraton Wall Centre whose staff stayed true to their word in providing "world-class" service. Every employee was empowered to help us. This meant we could stop any staff members in the hall at any time and they could discuss and change logistics, add refreshments or menu items, cut keys, give us complimentary parking passes and more. We knew we didn't need to spend time and energy chasing down the right person because any staff member had the ability to serve us. If employees had questions or needed to confirm things with a supervisor, they would immediately get back to us. To create **bold** service, staff needs to be empowered to assist clients.

GET STRAIGHT TO THE HEART OF SERVICE

Answer the question, "Why are we doing this?" for every problem, opportunity, policy or procedure. Many managers focus on training employees on how to do their jobs, but often neglect why the job needs to be done in the first place. You may have heard this before—"When you understand **why**, the **how** falls into place"—because motivation comes from understanding the purpose of our work. Have ongoing open conversations with employees about why service is important. As a group, discuss what good service looks like. See if employees can find examples of excellent service in action.

Final Thoughts

People keep the service mentality alive, so create a system that is flexible to allow them to do this. Have a clear and compelling vision that inspires. Finally, keep reinforcing this vision. Your **bold** service mentality will shine through.

ACTION PLAN

1. Understand the ten pitfalls of rules.

2. Empower employees to rely on their own judgment by asking, "What is the best way to handle this?"

3. Complete the five steps to create compassionate service systems.

4. Test your service mentality. Ask employees what the organization does. (Does service mentality shine?)

5. Communicate why rules and objectives are necessary.

6. Complete the two essential steps to cement your bold service mentality.

Chapter Five

Creating a Fun Workplace:
When Hokey Pokey *Is* "What It's All About"

- Learn the Thirty-one Ways to Have Fun at Work
- Understand the Benefits of Humor
- Test Your Workplace—Is Your Staff Suffering from Terminal Seriousness?
- Find Out How Humor Is Created
- Thirteen Steps to Creating a Fun Workplace

As the saying goes *all work and no play makes Jack a dull boy.* Do you want dull people working for you? Traditionally, work is not supposed to be fun. You spend 40 hours a week on average working—that's 1,840 hours a year (if you remove holidays), or 86,840 hours in your working life. (These facts are meant to inform, not to depress you.) Why can't our work be fun? The biggest argument against a "fun" workplace is that it's not *productive.*

HOW FUN IS PRODUCTIVE

Imagine a work world where people love their work environment, and they are calm, stress-free and happy all day long. People who are in good spirits are more likely to be productive. Their mental attitude produces increased oxygen, endorphins, and blood flow to the brain, which enables them to think more clearly and creatively. They are more relaxed, more accepting of others, and more likely to share their sense of humor.

Laughter creates a bond that brings others together; people like to be with employees who are having fun. Creativity, intuition and flexibility are key to successful operation of organizations today. In stimulating environments, employees enjoy their time at work and they will also excel at work. Attracting customers is easier in an environment of hospitality. A fun workplace is not only more productive, but it attracts people and profits.

A TEST: IS YOUR STAFF SUFFERING FROM TERMINAL SERIOUSNESS?

Scan your workplace and take note:

Do you regularly catch people laughing or smiling at work?

☐ YES ☐ NO

When something funny happens do people stop and appreciate it?

☐ YES ☐ NO

Does your organization have fun activities at least monthly?

☐ YES ☐ NO

Do you have tools (fun giveaways, draws) to invite clients to participate in having fun in your environment?

☐ YES   ☐ NO

Are managers usually optimistic and smiling at work?

☐ YES   ☐ NO

If you answer no to two or more of these questions, your staff probably suffers from "terminal seriousness," which is negatively affecting morale and productivity.

More Benefits of Humor in the Workplace

Dr. Norman Cousins said, "Laughter is an igniter of great expectations." Children laugh an average of 400 times a day and that number drops to only 15 times a day by the time people reach age 35. Preschoolers must know something we don't. Laughter releases endorphins (a chemical 10 times more powerful than the pain-relieving drug morphine) into the body with the same exhilarating effect as doing strenuous exercise. Laughing increases oxygen intake, thereby replenishing and invigorating cells. It also increases the pain threshold, boosts immunity, and relieves stress.

Humor also levels the playing field to create an atmosphere that encourages honest dialogue, open communication, and increased risk-taking. Creating more equality in power or control shows people respect and builds pride in their work.

This is just a sampling of the benefits of having fun in your workplace. Hopefully now you are convinced you could use a "fun injection" in your own place of employment. Read on to find out how to get started.

HOW HUMOR IS CREATED

Laughter and humor are different. The physical experience of laughter comes as a result of humor, so humor usually precedes laughter although it doesn't have to. Studies show that you can "fake it until you make it" and have the same physiological effects as a real laugh. If you suffer from terminal seriousness (or have some staff members that do), just start laughing and smiling for no reason at all and you will start to reap the rewards.

One theory on how humor is created is called the *Incongruity Theory.* This theory suggests that we laugh when two incongruent things come together unexpectedly. The laughter is the "Aha! I got it, aren't I clever" response to the humor. A good joke leads you in one direction and then turns abruptly in a completely opposite and unexpected direction. In an instant, the mind bounces from one reality to the next.

An example: I went to an unfinished furniture store and they sold me a tree.

What makes this joke funny is it leads you in one direction and then suddenly takes you in another. The punch line is unexpected.

HUMOR AND THE UNEXPECTED IN THE WORKPLACE

If humor is about the surprising or unexpected, how does this concept help you incorporate humor into your workplace? Humorous surprises will elicit fun. Imagine showing up for work wearing a clown nose and handing them out for others to enjoy. It would be fun to order a surprise pizza for lunch. It would be a pleasant surprise for some managers to tell a joke or smile once in awhile. Be on the look out for ways to do the unexpected.

You can also use the Incongruity Theory to change perspective by taking the tedium of daily issues and lightening them up with an unexpected twist.

Exercise: Take a stressful issue in your workplace and challenge it with humor. Have your employees exaggerate and look for the surprising and funny in everyday challenging events. Stress usually comes from your perspective and a negative perspective may undergo an adjustment when you introduce humor.

THIRTEEN STEPS TO CREATING A FUN WORKPLACE:

1. Give up the notion that professionalism means being serious all the time. It's possible to take yourself lightly and still be competent and productive. Start to promote the benefits of humor at work.

2. Define what *fun is* in your workplace and what it *is not* (e.g. harmful humor, off-color jokes, sexual humor, humor tarnishing the organization)

3. Organize a "Fun Committee" for dreaming up fun "stuff" to do during and after work.

4. Add fun to meetings. Bring in fun things such as Nerf balls, a basketball and hoop, or party blowers. Start a meeting with a humorous story or joke.

5. Collect and share your favorite cartoons and jokes. Create a **Joke Board** or a **Humor Newsletter**. Look for tools to disseminate fun and funny things daily.

6. Let customers know you are a **fun** company. Do something just for fun (organize fun customer events, dress for fun, share funny things with customers) and give employees tools to create a fun relationship with customers (stickers, candy for children, dog biscuits for dogs, humorous buttons with the company logo). This makes work more fun for employees and it strengthens the relationship with customers. Dick Snow of *Ben and Jerry's Ice Cream* says, "We believe that we're in the entertainment business and selling ice cream is just a part of what we do. In our stores the counter is our stage and the customers are our audience." Disneyland has the same kind of approach. Employees are part of an entertainment experience, and they aren't just doing a job.

7. Gather your co-workers for the "Joy of Work" hour. Everyone must talk about something good at work. Take turns telling stories about the things that make work a joy. Each person should contribute ideas on how to make work more fun.

8. Have a fun recognition program. Fun is not a reward for performance, but can be a way to encourage employees to perform. For example, you could create "games" out of productive activity…who can motivate the most patients in a hospital to smile and say something funny to the head nurse. Playful and goal-oriented fun is best.

9. Respond to fun when it happens. Funny things occur all the time, but if you are obsessed with left-brain analytical thought, you might find it hard to stop and respond. Natural spontaneous humor is a blessing. Stop and take a moment to give employees and customers an opportunity to see the fun in the event.

10. Commit to being fun and it will change your approach to work. Start slowly with a few activities and communicate your desire to create a more relaxed workplace. Don't expect things to turn around overnight.

11. Put fun things and activities in the staff room. This allows people to take their mind off of the seriousness of work for a short period, so they come back to work with a more positive and balanced perspective.

12. Encourage staff to leave work behind at the end of the day. Employees shouldn't be so consumed with work that it affects their family life and leisure activities. Find fun ways for employees to "unload" at the end of the day or week. Create a ritual like writing a "to do" list and posting it on the board. By doing this, you commit to not thinking about the things on the list until the next day.

13. Encourage employees to develop their own style of having fun. A nurse anesthetist at a hospital in Michigan often sings to his patients to help them relax prior to surgery. Patients have appreciated this so much that they have told family and friends about the experience. It is not uncommon now for the hospital staff to get requests for "The Singing Anesthesiologist" when they are scheduling their surgery.

Remember that employees create fun in the workplace, not managers. It's a manager's job to orchestrate fun activities (and not get in the way of them).

Even bad news can be delivered in a more fun way to lessen the negativity of the information. If you need to remind employees or customers with signs, then word them in a fun and humorous way. To remind employees to fill out their time sheets, instead of posting a negative sign such as, "If you don't fill out your time sheets you don't get paid," try wording it in a humorous way. "If you love your job so much you don't want us to pay you, then don't fill out your timesheet."

THIRTY-ONE WAYS TO HAVE FUN AT WORK

1. Minigolf in the office.

2. Have **joy breaks**. Stock the staff room with "fun" toys (Silly Putty, building blocks, Frisbees, Slinky).

3. Create a humorous company salute.

4. Print fun greeting cards for employees to give to customers.

5. Charge late employees a small fine like $5, which goes to fun activities.

6. Plan office parties.

7. Wear fun clothes.

8. Have "Fun Awards."

9. Pass out homemade cookies or chocolate.

10. Give Christmas gifts to employees.

11. Celebrate the seasons (Valentine cards, Hanukkah gifts, Christmas carols, April Fools jokes, St. Patrick's Day, Easter egg hunt).

12. Have a theme day. Encourage staff to dress up.

13. Have a massage therapist provide shoulder massages for people at their workstations.

14. Wash all employees' cars in the parking lot.

15. Create and distribute fun stories from within the organization.

16. Play charades.

17. Name rooms in your department after staff members.

18. Have employees bring photos of their children to work.

19. Display photos of staff events.

20. Hang unique artwork.

21. Have an employee fun day.

22. Bring creative events to the business (e.g. A scavenger hunt).

23. Play office Jeopardy or Bingo.

24. Invent contests.

25. Bring Nerf balls, foam darts, a basketball hoop.

26. Supply a plastic bowling set.

27. Have employees create a list of fun things to do.

28. Offer relay races.

29. Stage marshmallow fights.

30. Have a fun pass: This person is eligible to have fun by_____(fill in activity).

31. Make "Stop Being So Serious" awards.

ACTION PLAN

1. Remember—fun is productive.

2. Use the incongruity theory to inject humor into everyday stress-inducing events.

3. Decide if your staff suffers from terminal seriousness.

4. Define humor in your workplace.

5. Create a "Fun Committee."

6. Incorporate at least **five** of the **thirty-one** ways to have fun at work.

Chapter Six

For the Good of the Group

How to Encourage Cooperation over Competition

- Develop a Spirit of Cooperation in Your Workplace
- Determine If Your Acknowledgment Program Is Causing Competition
- Find Out If Favoritism Is Hurting Your Team
- Ensure Jobs Are Designed for Function and Not Power

Are You Creating Unnecessary Competition in Your Workplace?

Some competition is healthy, but in most organizations it's not. When you have to get along and work together, the act of pitting people against one another is dangerous. When surpassing others is more important than doing a good job, quality will suffer. If employees get wrapped up in competition, they will lose focus. Imagine if you could channel that same energy towards cooperating and meeting shared objectives.

Cooperation should be valued over competition because teams are far more powerful than individuals.

Three Factors That Create Competition in Your Workplace:

1. Your acknowledgment program.

2. Showing favoritism to certain employees.

3. Emphasizing imbalances in power.

Your Acknowledgment Program

Healthy competition or hoarding heroic praise?

When your star employees consistently bask in the spotlight, the motivation and determination of other staff members suffer. Everyone loses. A team environment counts on individuals working for the good of the group. This means that the super-stars who love hoarding praise will spoil a team environment. Competition arises when people are set apart. Unfortunately, most generic award programs do exactly that. (See *Chapter Two—Caught in the Act.*)

Is your acknowledgment program causing competition?

- Are the same "stars" continually acknowledged and usually selected for promotions?

- Does your performance appraisal program lack elements that focus on teamwork?

If you answered yes to either of these questions, then your award program is causing unnecessary competition.

When you need people to cooperate as a team, consider rewarding cooperation and not competition. Start by giving awards and performance appraisals to teams, not individuals. Recognize employees who help others get things done or who work in the interest of the whole group. Cooperation is about working together in shared purpose.

HOW TO EMPHASIZE COOPERATION OVER COMPETITION

1. Emphasize team accountability over individual performance.

Some workforces can be reorganized to emphasize team accountability over individual production. Start by creating a team objective instead of individual objectives and keep the focus on team performance. In this way, employees aren't competing against each other, but strengthening their colleagues' efforts. Look at your current objectives and ask, "Which ones could be made into team objectives?"

2. Cooperation is about working together in shared purpose.

Managers should regularly look for opportunities to link individual performance to the good of the group. Emphasize group purpose in coaching sessions, in your acknowledgment program, in performance appraisals, in newsletters and at meetings.

3. Keep the big picture front and center.

Go through each job function with your employees and ask, "How does this role link to (and help accomplish) the organization's mission, vision and values?" Once you have answers, communicate them often.

4. Competition with other units or departments.

Is your department deemed superior to other departments? Some organizations inadvertently encourage status perceptions and it can be harmful to the overall organization. Keep communication open between departments and let employees work in other departments for a while. They will become ambassadors for each department and be a driving force to make them cohesive.

Showing Favoritism to Certain Employees

Favoritism directly encourages competition and destroys cooperation. Favoritism in the workplace is quite common. If managers are in a position to grant employees opportunities, what's to stop them from showing preference to people they like? Managers may not even consciously realize they are being preferential. By nature, we are drawn to some people more than others because we share similar likes, dislikes or backgrounds.

Consider this example: A manager hires someone qualified for the job. After getting to know each other, these two people realize they both have a lot in common: both grew up on farms, they married their high school sweethearts, and they both like drinking rye and coke. Pretty soon, a bond forms. Everyone in the office can tell these two folks get along really well. Everyone will also soon notice if more challenging and interesting work goes to the friend because he and the manager are alike.

Pitfalls to Showing Favoritism:

- In some cases it's illegal.

- Employees will resent you.

- Employees learn not to trust you.

- It's unfair to be judged by individual likability.

- It creates tension with other staff members.

- It harms your credibility.

Most people get a job thinking the most important measure of their success is performance. If they discover that managers are acknowledging, favoring or even promoting people just because they get along well with each other, the performance personnel will lose motivation. It also blurs the lines; employees will wonder what is important in this organization— performance or getting on well with the boss?

STEPS TO CONTROL FAVORITISM IN THE WORKPLACE

1. When opportunities for special projects or advancement arise, be fair. Every employee with the right skills should be considered. Organizations need a process for internal promotions to make sure all candidates know of the opportunity and are treated fairly when they apply.

2. It is valuable if more than one person can be involved with internal promotions.

3. If you think you might be showing favoritism to someone, ask yourself, "Does this person make a good point, or do I just want him to be right?"

4. Managers should be aware of how often they acknowledge certain employees over others and consciously create a balance.

Competitive Employees

Some people are born to be competitive. A problem develops when they steal the thunder from others, exaggerate results or withhold information. Some competition can be very healthy and motivating. Control aggressive competition, however, by recognizing it, and addressing it immediately. If someone exaggerates results, have her give evidence. If an employee withholds information, have him bring that information forward (privately, not publicly). Then say something like, "I know you are competitive, but I would like that competition to work for the good of the group." Try not to establish too many competitive situations (e.g. best sales awards) and finally, always link individual behavior to the overall contribution to the group.

Employees Who Demand Lots of Attention

Some employees crowd you for every ounce of your attention. Thwart these personal cheerleading attempts by demanding performance *first*. Recognition follows as a natural reward. It is not necessary to acknowledge employees for work they are supposed to do anyway. Look for opportunities to show approval, but be very specific about what you are praising, and link the individual's behavior to the good of the group. Be careful to acknowledge everyone. Don't focus all your kind words on those who leap out for approval.

EMPHASIZING IMBALANCES IN POWER:
Designing Jobs for Power or Function?

Jobs that emphasize power insist there are lines of communication and protocol that must be obeyed. Often employees with more power will oversee or approve others' work. Sometimes, such as in the case of dealing with a new employee, it is necessary to supervise daily operations, but excessive management disintegrates team spirit and stimulates unhealthy competition.

The Test

For every supervisory or management role ask, "Is this position necessary for power or function?"

It's "functional" if the person overseeing the work is able to contribute to the overall process. If supervision is just a way to maintain control or power then the job should be redesigned. Everyone on the team should be contributing to the overall good of the project.

HOW TO BUILD A SPIRIT OF COOPERATION

Large organizations often have units or departments that operate in almost complete isolation from other departments. Yet they have a lot in common. They share mission, vision, values, products, services and more. Because of this isolation, many employees don't get to feel as attached or committed to the final product. Some departments may not even see the final product. No matter how large an organization, it is a mistake to allow departments to operate in isolation. Employees should feel part of the overall direction of the organization.

Why not encourage all departments to build a spirit of cooperation throughout the organization?

Some Ways to Accomplish Interdepartmental Cooperation

- Events

- Cross-training in other departments

- Interdepartmental visits

- Cross-departmental recognition vehicles (i.e. vouchers that can be given to employees in other departments)

- Newsletters highlighting the achievements of other departments

- Have an employee give a speech in another department

ACTION PLAN

1. Develop elements in your rewards program that emphasize teamwork.

2. Eliminate rewards that cause competition.

3. Develop ways to emphasize group purpose.

4. Reassess your internal promotions system to eliminate favoritism.

5. For every job or role, ask, "Is this job designed for power or function?"

Chapter Seven

Lessons in Linguistic Chivalry:
How to Create a Listening Culture

- Four Common Listening Challenges
- How to Listen Actively
- Exercises in the ABCs of Effective Listening
- How to Manage for Consensus

Lousy Listeners Slaughter Enthusiasm

We approached our manager to share our ideas. Within minutes he cut off our thoughts, slaughtering our enthusiasm. Like an autocratic parent, he stripped the vitality from our ideas. Worse, he couldn't even feign enough dignity to pretend to listen. Instead, he waited for his opportunity to talk and formulated his response while we spoke. We felt like children begging against our parents' will.

Ideas carry with them enthusiasm. When employees' ideas are disregarded, it endangers their existence; they quickly learn to guard their ideas and limit their input. The job becomes *All Work & No Say*. This stifles creativity, risk taking, enthusiasm, passion and productivity. The well of ideas and enthusiasm evaporates. Employees at all levels need to be heard and listened to in order to feel that they belong and have significance and respect.

IGNORANCE BREEDS IGNORANCE

The workplace is rife with opportunities for ignorance. When managers ignore their staff, a chain reaction occurs: employees ignore customers; customers ignore their contracts and sales plummet. Embroiled in the link is the need to be heard. Ignorance begets ignorance. Ignore one person's thoughts and they will ignore yours. Assumptions will fester, employees will misinterpret facts, agendas will become frustrated and people will lose their impetus to fuel their ideas. Enthusiasm is crushed and careers crash and crumble.

Managers who unveil the new scheme of things without corralling staff input should expect mediocre results. Employees are responsible for results. To get their buy-in you need their input.

Are people ignoring each other on purpose? Perhaps, because it has become acceptable in the work culture. Part of the puzzle is to develop simple listening skills. Everyone from managers to line employees should make listening a priority.

A TEST: ARE YOU A LOUSY LISTENER?
RANK YOUR LISTENING SKILLS

To find out how others perceive your listening skills, ask two or three colleagues to anonymously answer the following survey:

On a scale of 1 to 5, give the listener a score as follows: 1=Never, 2=Rarely, 3=Sometimes, 4=Often, 5=Very Often.

1. This colleague interrupts my conversation.

2. This colleague talks more than listens.

3. This colleague often is distracted while I speak, multitasking or doing something else.

4. This colleague doesn't indicate he has heard what I said.

5. This colleague jumps to conclusions or tries to immediately solve my problems.

6. I often don't feel heard by this person.

I suggest that if you score **over 14**, there is **room for improvement** in your listening skills. Practice the ABCs of Listening exercises below and than have two or three other anonymous colleagues do this quiz until your listening score is averaging below 12. Managers should survey the listening skills of each staff member. You may also want clients to fill out a similar listening survey to check how your staff's listening skills fare with clients.

FOUR COMMON LISTENING CHALLENGES

Being distracted: The classic Type A personality. This type is often caught doing two or three things at once and listens this way, too. This listener's attention is easily distracted by other stimuli. This kills the life expectancy of a conversation and trains others to be short with their words. Listening requires a single-minded focus.

Jumping to conclusions: Some people are masters at frustrating a conversation by jumping to conclusions and bringing the conversation to an abrupt halt. Remember most people think two to three times faster than others can speak. Don't get caught in the trap of using that extra time to form your own conclusions.

Pretending to listen: Lousy listeners train themselves to pretend to listen. Meanwhile, their minds are really racing ahead with their own schedule of thoughts. These listeners cover up their deception with a false "Uh huh, right, I see..." or nod their heads as though they agree. The problem is some gullible employees may believe they have their co-workers support and understanding, only to be misled. We listen faster than we speak, so you need to train yourself to pay attention and not let the mind wander.

Interrupting others: Some people habitually interrupt others, snatching the moment to stomp ahead with their point. Others have to clamor to get a word in edgewise and creativity stumbles. Priorities synchronize only when both parties are committed to paying attention. Conversation "hogs" would be wise to learn some linguistic chivalry.

Lousy listeners are enthralled by their own words while their co-workers feel handcuffed to the conversation, suffering in silence.

FOUR STEPS TO ACTIVE LISTENING

1. **Hearing:** At this stage, you simply pay attention to make sure you hear the message.

2. **Feedback and interpretation:** If you fail to interpret a speaker's words correctly it leads to misunderstanding. Confirm you heard what was said by feeding back questions until what the person is saying matches what you understand. Questions confirm your understanding (or lack of it). They also let people know you heard them correctly.

3. **Evaluation:** Decide what to do with the information you have received.

4. **Response:** This is a verbal or visual cue to the speaker whether you have understood the message.

Avoid offering solutions too early: Many people just want to be heard; they simply need to vent. Offering a solution too soon will frustrate them. By talking out loud, people often solve their own problems anyway. Be careful not to jump in and provide a solution too early. Hear them out and only offer a solution if you think it will help.

Check your body language: Your body language gives away your intention to listen. A poor listener's body language will eventually betray her listening level because 80% of all communication shows up in body language. Active listening requires that you lean forward, even mirroring the speaker's posture. Maintain eye contact and nod with agreement to encourage speakers to go on.

Listen for key ideas: Some folks ramble with little direction. Don't be discouraged; active listening requires groping for key points and mentally pegging important ideas. Help keep the conversation moving with verbal encouragements ("OK, yes... go on"), and open-ended questions ("What did he say? How come? Who was involved?")

Listen and watch for nonverbal clues to meaning: Many messages are communicated nonverbally by tone of voice, facial expression, posture, energy level, and behavior patterns. Studies show that the nonverbal clues may be more important than the verbal.

Avoid dead-end questions: If you want to get people talking, ask them questions that encourage interaction. Questions that require a yes or no answer lead a conversation to a dead end.

Focus on content not delivery: Here's a quick test! When you're listening, are you distracted by how often someone:

- says "Um, ah…yeah" or other repeated phrases?

- paces?

- bites his fingernails or plays with her hair?

If so, then you are focusing on delivery, not content.

Speak the same language: A listening technique that strengthens employee confidence in their ideas is to feed back their own phrasing or terms. In that way, they know their ideas are being listened to and valued.

Present for consensus: Instead of presenting ideas, ask for buy-in. Instead of saying, "Here is what is going to happen," present it as, "Here is what we are considering. What do you think?"

Suspend judgment: Imagine a co-worker has capsized a conversation and is flaunting her authority while you are the innocent listener. Her bristling words are hard not to judge. Yes, some conversations are more exhausting than others. Regardless of the speaker's aggressive ways, do your best to suspend judgment and keep the conversation moving along. When you find yourself judging someone's perspective, take a step back and judge the content of the message rather than the speaker.

Paraphrase and ask questions: To paraphrase is to summarize a speaker's message and show them that you fully understand their meaning. "OK, Bob, I hear you saying that you're not happy with the scheduling around here." Then ask questions like, "What do you propose we do about it?" or "Are you suggesting we...?" These questions lead to clarification and buy-in from Bob.

Empathize with the speaker: Often people just want to be heard. They may not even want any action or resolution. Before immediately offering solutions to their problems, just listen and show empathy. An example is, "Bob, I can relate. The scheduling is hard on us and I understand your frustrations." Always respond to feelings first and then to facts.

Don't believe everything you hear: Active listening doesn't mean you have to believe everything others say. Don't lead people on to make them think you agree with them if you don't. Show you have heard what's been said and state your point of view. A lot of conversation is often wrapped in ego, opinions, and judgment, so try to separate the "fact from the fever" and don't be persuaded by the approach. Instead, listen for factual ideas and act on these.

Agreeing with someone's point of view isn't necessary but understanding them is.

EXERCISING THE ABC'S OF EFFECTIVE LISTENING

The following are listening exercises to practice with your staff:

Exercise A: Practice paraphrasing. One person talks while the other actively listens and then paraphrases what is said. Remember to empathize and include the other person's point of view.

Exercise B: Discussion partners A and B. A facilitator talks about something for about 5 minutes. Partner A tells partner B what has been said. Partner B adds anything that has been missed. Both partners practice good listening.

Exercise C: Ask questions to clarify. Sometimes people neglect to ask questions because they are afraid the answer is too obvious. Practice role-playing where the facilitator explains something, but doesn't give all the details. Practice asking questions to clarify the information. If people nod in agreement and nobody comes forth with questions or ask only the obvious, then start questioning them. "So what do you think I meant by...?" If participants give you blank looks, you know your workplace needs to encourage people to ask questions when in doubt. Start by encouraging this to happen in the future and perhaps rewarding it when it does.

Don't Tell Them, Ask Them— A Formula for Effective Management

For managers, listening is sometimes more important than telling because people respond better when they feel included. This is a dramatic shift for some managers, so it requires practice. A good management training activity is to role-play by turning directives or commands (telling others what to do) into asking others to do things that go above and beyond their call of duty.

For instance, instead of saying, "I need you to be more productive," ask, "How can I help you be more productive?" Or "How can we be more productive?" Sometimes, it is just a simple matter of phrasing what you say as a question.

Asking is a very powerful tool but **only** when it is acceptable for employees *not* to do something you are asking them to do. You don't want to have to ask employees to do things that are part of their job description. Managers need to strike a good balance between asking and telling.

MANAGING FOR CONSENSUS

A leader's job is also to enhance organizational adaptability. You do this by managing for consensus. The surest way to get others to buy into organizational ideas and objectives is to make those ideas their own. Get employees buy-in to ensure success because people are much more responsive and responsible when it's their ideas on the line.

**Implement methods that help regularly gauge
and listen to employee input:**

- You could try monthly focus groups and invite all staff to participate;

- Tie input to group performance and acknowledgment programs;

- Have an implementation newsletter to keep employees informed;

- Have an "ideas and efficiency session" once a month where employees are expected to show up with new ideas they have and talk about how they implemented ideas last month.

- Practice the ABC's of Listening exercises with your staff

Even if employees can't have **say** in the creation of policies or objectives, they can have **say** in the implementation. And they should. After all, frontline employees know the day-to-day business better than anyone else does. It's the consensus of the group that is important, not the policy itself.

Don't bother trying to gain consensus just for the purpose of gaining consensus because employees will be wise to your ways.

Banishing Business as Usual

When good listening is a part of the day-to-day culture at work, it squashes the "ho hum business as usual" attitude. Conversations will be fueled with passion for the work. People feel respected for their contributions and are willing to give their best. Work can be dull for those who are neither committed nor passionate. In a listening culture, these dull candidates will not be able to hide their apathy. The spirited and impassioned employees will prevail.

ACTION PLAN:

1. Practice the four keys to active listening.

2. Look for common listening challenges in your employees.

3. Practice the ABCs of effective listening.

Chapter Eight

How to Stop Micromanaging and Start Delegating

- Are You Micromanaging Your Staff?
- The Pitfalls of Micromanaging
- How to Delegate to the Right People
- Five Steps to Delegate Well
- How to Deal with Mistakes without Destroying Confidence
- When Employees Catch Their Colleagues Making Mistakes

Oversteering the Project: A Collision Course

Excessive monitoring of employees' daily tasks will generate ill feelings. Imagine this: a manager badgers an employee to take on a project. The ambitious employee obliges, but must endure the manager's meddling with every detail. This trap only has to open and shut once for the employee to conclude that it's exhausting to take on new projects.

Some managers make the mistake of micromanaging their employees' work. They regularly step in and try to control the process or the outcome, doing more harm than good.

Pitfalls to Micromanaging

Micromanaging creates extra work. To be involved, managers will need to be in the know. Who is taking care of what? Where is the information? What agreements (oral, written and understood) have been made? If you don't know this you may end up frustrating many people and creating a lot of work for yourself.

When a manager steps in and takes charge it makes the baffled employee wonder, "Is this still my role? What am I responsible for now?" Co-workers will wonder to which project director they're obliged to direct inquiries, information, or customers.

Meddling conveys a lack of trust. Those under scrutiny will be less likely to take risks, will doubt themselves and proceed more cautiously before taking initiative.

HOW TO DELEGATE TO THE RIGHT PEOPLE

To effectively delegate you have to learn to manage the different styles in your workforce. Someone else's approach may differ from the thoughts and processes you hold, but that doesn't make them wrong.

Before delegating a project, you need to know two key details:

1. The personality traits best suited for this project.

2. The problem-solving strengths of each of your staff members.

How to Delegate to the Right People: A List of Considerations

Time Management. People manage time differently. Some feel compelled to do a task right away or it won't get done. If you are working on a short-term project that needs to be completed very quickly, this individual is naturally your best choice. Others manage a project towards longer deadlines and still others meander around details for months and race to complete the project before deadline.

What kind of time management does your project require?

The Bigger Picture. Some folks are great at managing details, but when it comes to the "big picture," they shy away. Others will suffocate in too much detail but are great at overseeing ideas. If you choose someone who is detail-oriented, you will have to provide the big picture. Conversely, if you choose someone who is a big picture thinker they may need support in managing the details.

Direction and Support. Some employees will plow through a project with very little guidance from you. Others continually barrage you with questions in search of guidance and recognition. Decide how much guidance you are willing or able to give to the project and how much you need to control the outcome. Some projects you can just "hand over" to others, but others require constant reinforcement.

Clearly Defined Outcomes. When you delegate, ensure that person or team is well briefed regarding specific outcomes. Leaving the project to open interpretation will invite your criticism when you discover the outcome does not match your expectations. Agree upon specific outcomes at the beginning of the project.

To enable someone else to do the job for you, you must ensure that:

- they know what to do.

- they know how to do it.

- they have the authority to achieve it.

By giving others authority, a manager does not lose control, he gains it. Empowering people makes the manager and the organization stronger. Leaders cannot be in two places at once and the more authority others have, the quicker they are able to respond to situations and events.

SEVEN TIPS FOR EFFECTIVE DELEGATING

1. Be clear on the task that needs to be accomplished, the skills required to see it through, and your best people for the job.

2. Set outcomes, objectives and timelines.

3. Communicate how much support and feedback the employees can expect.

4. Make it clear to employees that their customers (or projects) are their responsibility.

5. Don't step in and take over unless it's absolutely necessary.

6. Establish deadlines and maintain regular updates that ensure things are being completed.

7. Manage the bigger picture. Take a step back and manage the overall vision to make sure things happen through others.

Ensure that clients know your employees will take care of them. If a client complains about an employee, the temptation is for a manager is to step in and fix the situation. Direct the client back to the employee they are working with. Discuss your concerns with the employee and ask or suggest how they can better manage the situation. You may need to be involved in a meeting with the employee and the client.

Stepping on Toes

Sometimes you have no choice but to step in. Someone may be incompetent, slacking off, or just unable to manage the work-load and you don't want business or customers to suffer. However, be careful not to diminish an already weakened staff member. To make the process smoother:

1. **Talk** with the employee and explain you are going to help out and why. Work to gain their acceptance, so they will be helpful in the transition.

2. **Gather** as much information as possible about what has been done so far, what commitments were made and to whom.

3. **Re-delegate** or complete the project yourself. Ask first, "Can I delegate this?" because you may find yourself overwhelmed with work.

4. **Communicate** the change to customers and co-workers.

You Light the Flame and I'll Carry the Torch

Delegating a project means making sure employees get full credit for their contributions. Managers should never take credit for the work of others. Employees deserve full credit. People don't want to work hard just to enrich the boss's image.

Dealing with Mistakes without Destroying Someone's Confidence

Part of delegating is to recognize that people will make mistakes when wading into new and unfamiliar territory. Errors occur for many reasons, including unclear instruction, inadequate feedback or insufficient authority to get the job done. Many aren't the fault of the employees, but of managers for not being prepared to delegate in the first place. If employees are afraid to come forward with mistakes, what do they do instead? Cover them up. Instead of being able to learn from their mistakes, employees pretend they didn't happen. As the cover-up deepens, so does the damage it causes.

GIVING FEEDBACK ON INADEQUATE PERFORMANCE

Your goals are to:

1. help the stymied staff member understand the problem.

2. give them the confidence to do it better next time.

3. make sure it doesn't happen again.

Remember: Never reprimand others for things beyond their control.

Solutions-oriented Not Problem Focused

Whether it's good or bad, behavior that gets recognized gets repeated. Managers may spend most of their time focusing on a problem, sometimes at the expense of the solution. Being solutions-oriented means recognizing the problem and why it occurred, then immediately shifting gears towards a solution. What will we do differently in the future? To give employees the confidence to improve, you need to believe more in them than they believe in themselves. An employee who has just made a mistake may feel embarrassed and lack confidence in his own abilities, which can have a downward spiraling effect on performance. If a manager can restore an employee's confidence, the long-term benefits are a stronger relationship between them and a greater commitment for the employee to the job.

ARE YOU CREATING A CLIMATE OF BLAME?

When Employees Catch Their Colleagues Making Mistakes

Mistakes should be reported and dealt with. Often those in the front lines notice errors first. Many organizations use peer reporting and this can cause a climate of blame. Employees are actually out to catch their co-workers making mistakes. It makes sense to have employees report performance mistakes, but you need to establish some ground rules.

1. Errors should be specific. Colleagues should only report on errors in the tangible aspects of another's work. Don't accept or solicit personal opinions or generalities such as "Mike just isn't a team player."

2. When possible, encourage employees to go directly to the person making the mistake and offer help. Some training on explaining errors to others may be in order. Make sure employees know "blame is not the game" and the goal is to be aware of where mistakes are happening and lending assistance to mend them. When a mistake is reported, don't treat it like a bad thing but as an opportunity to do it right the next time.

3. Allow employees to learn from each other's mistakes. If mistakes are treated as opportunities to learn and grow, people shouldn't be fearful of coming forward when they make them. When mistakes are openly communicated, others learn from them and avoid making the same mistake. This also creates a climate that encourages others to come forward with questions to avoid errors happening in the future.

ACTION PLAN

1. Make sure you delegate to the right person.

2. Plan the amount of direction, support, feedback and follow-up you will provide.

3. Make sure employees have the authority to do the job.

4. Be solutions-oriented, not problem-focused, when dealing with mistakes.

Chapter Nine

Managing the Emotional Workplace

How to Create an Emotionally Responsible and Engaging Workplace

- What Aggravates Emotions in Your Workplace?
- How to Create a Culture of Responsible Emotional Management
- How to Create an Emotionally Engaging Workplace

He wears a permanent stern scowl. Each line is carved from years of experience in the corporate trenches. He's put in his time and his rough demeanor proves it. Nobody dares challenge his position or lack of charm. He has earned the right to be a grouch. In the meantime, his co-workers suffer daily from his sorry disposition. But what lies beneath his professional façade? Fear. He fears change, being replaced or becoming obsolete.

Emotional Management

It happens to all of us. Emotions crowd the mind, slowly bubbling outwards to disrupt our jobs. Be it fear, rage, jealousy, competition, defensiveness, emotions dwell with us in the workplace. Below are samplings of familiar scenarios:

- Employees who occasionally burst into fits of rage.

- Employees devoid of all feelings and emotionally detached.

- Competitive employees, who withhold information, exaggerate results and cheat others in order to look good.

- Employees who demand attention and recognition even for mediocre results.

- Control freaks or manipulators who deceive others to gain the upper hand.

Do any of these symptoms sound familiar in your workplace? If so, read on.

SIX FORCES THAT AGGRAVATE EMOTIONS IN YOUR WORKPLACE

There are forces in your workplace that could be causing negative emotions to build up and affect performance and morale:

1. Rules that Mask Emotion

Rules and policies can strangle employees. Some work can also be sterile, technical and at times unfulfilling. Repetitive work especially tends to engender complacency. Humans need to express their emotions. Since most full-time employees spend the bulk of their day at work, you would expect them to take ownership and pride in something that consumes so much of their time. If that ownership is threatened (by other employees, changing policies, re-assigned projects, etc.), they may revolt and emotions will flare.

2. Controlling Managers

Management style really affects emotions. Autocratic styles don't fare well because these managers demand obedience and expect employees to do only as they are told. If employees feel they are under constant surveillance, they learn to react and become defensive about their work.

3. Robbing Employees of Positive Recognition

Employees aren't at their best at all times. If they are caught in the act of doing less-than-average work, when normally their standards are higher, they may lash out in defense. Since many jobs aren't project-based, they have no beginning and no end; therefore, they offer no regular feeling of accomplishment on completion. Employees may feel cheated of recognition and support from management.

4. Guarding Information

Information is power. Some employees may guard information as a form of control. Again, if this information is threatened, they may revolt. This may show up in anger, resentment, defensiveness, ploys for attention, and emotional outbursts. Employees who don't have access to information also resent the being left out of knowledge given to others. Employees may feel they are victims rather than team members.

5. When People Don't Feel Heard

If employees feel their ideas aren't important or respected then negative emotions will fester. Staff members may decide that they will just do the bare minimum because anything above this will not be appreciated. When people do a good job and don't get recognized, resentment builds.

6. Beastly Bosses on the Edge of Influence

Unfortunately, many employees have not had training in people skills, teamwork, communication or personality styles. The result is that too often, workers who rise to a position of influence have less than perfect communication skills. Most managers don't get promoted to management level solely because of their communication skills or charm. They get promoted foremost because of their technical abilities. Ultimately, some great employees make horrible managers.

Anyone promoted to management should have their communications skills objectively assessed by numerous key employees. Most people don't leave a company: they leave their manager. One of the quickest ways to lose talented and resourceful employees is to have them report to emotionally volatile managers. Managers need to be very skilled at handling their emotions and communicating them.

Remember, you can't punish someone for his personality. For example, the nature of some employees is to be competitive; in fact, that may be why you hired them in the first place. Many emotional tendencies aren't challenged and go unexpressed until the next outburst. To fully engage employees in their work, we need to understand and recognize the way they feel.

HOW TO CREATE AN EMOTIONALLY ENGAGING WORKPLACE:

- Encourage open expression. Emotions, if denied, build up and suddenly explode. It's important to clear the air and remove emotional blocks by permitting the safe expression of feelings and emotions. Encourage employees to express their emotions regularly in a positive and constructive way.

- Provide venues for expression. If employees feel hurt, anger, resentment, etc., give them a venue to express themselves (a discussion box, a note to the manager, small informal focus groups, or a newsletter to discuss issues). Allow employees a means to contribute anonymously.

- Keep a thermometer of emotions at work. Regularly bring workplace "issues" out into the open. If your staff dislikes the new flexible work schedules, encourage them to express their feelings. Through discussion groups, meetings, etc. get a sense of the emotions at work. Even if you can't solve their problems, hearing people out will make them feel like they are important and will help them focus on their work.

- Make sure you have a solid and consistent recognition program. Managers should recognize employees on a regular basis. It can be informal and based on specific things managers catch employees doing well.

- Deal with emotional outbreaks. If cynical attitudes are running high at work, deal with them. Encourage emotional employees to discuss outbursts. Why are they upset and what will you do about it?

The Detached and Complacent Employee

The best way to pull people out of their complacency is to involve them. Make employees responsible for their opinions, actions and ideas. Give them a project to work on or something to commit to, or just draw out their opinions. Again, complacency may be an issue because employees are not challenged by their work, so make them responsible for a project or an outcome.

DEALING WITH MANIPULATIVE PEOPLE

Manipulation is a highly effective psychological weapon because it is not obvious. This is why manipulators are so powerful; you don't know you are being manipulated until it is too late. All of us have weaknesses that a cunning manipulator can exploit. Be aware of these weaknesses, so that you recognize when you are being manipulated. For instance, some people have a need to be liked and they can't handle criticism. The attentive manipulator will prey on this need by suggesting certain actions can lead to being disliked.

Recognize aggressive agendas. Look for a theme. Where do manipulators strike most often? Once you figure out these themes, you can convey your observations. "Greg, I hear you saying that you're not able to take on this project and you want me to handle it. What I don't appreciate is your suggestion that our relationship will be affected if I don't help you." Manipulation is indirect. The best way to squash it is to be direct.

If Jane harbors resentment for her co-worker, Mark, who has more power? Mark does. Jane gives power to Mark by allowing herself to be angry with him. It's a case of simple psychology at work. Truly powerful people are responsible for their own emotions. They won't allow people and experiences around them to seize control. It doesn't mean their emotions don't exist; they just refuse to let emotions ruin their day.

Emotions Are Beautiful

The fact that you have an animated workforce is a benefit. Clients prefer to deal with genuine people who respond with empathy and who value relationships. Computers can't do this. It's emotions that make us human. Our emotions are social sensors and a means of personal protection. Without emotions, our lives would be nondescript and boring.

Emotions are not wrong; it's what we do with them that can have repercussions. It's natural to be angry or competitive, but it's not natural to lash out in order to destroy someone's self-esteem. Remember computers are interchangeable and replaceable, but people are not. Replace a computer and nobody will notice, but replace a good employee and customers and co-workers are sure to have something to say.

ACTION PLAN

1. Assess the six factors that aggravate emotions in your workplace.

2. Deal with detached and complacent employees.

3. Deal with manipulative people.

4. Remember that emotions are beautiful.

Chapter Ten

Fierce Resolve

How to Engage Employees in Your Organization's Philosophy

- Learn the Six Steps to Make Organizational Philosophy Real
- Pitfalls to Corporate Philosophies, Values, Mission and Vision Statements
- How to Engage Employees in Your Organization's Philosophy
- How to Test Your Organization's Mission Statement
- Four Steps to Make Values Real to Employees

IF THE SHOE DOESN'T FIT:
When Philosophies Don't Engage the Employee

Imagine a company with very promising and fashionable but unrealistic philosophies about customer service, integrity and trust. What's wrong with having glorious ideals in the workplace? Like ill-fitting shoes, no one enjoys them. Many companies invest a lot of time and resources to develop corporate philosophies (corporate mission, vision and value statements), but employees don't buy into them because they just don't fit the actual job. In fact, some employees find these corporate philosophies poorly constructed and irritating. Why?

Often mission, vision and value statements are ambiguous. A new employee may be expected to absorb certain corporate philosophies he feels even the manager doesn't believe or understand. Sometimes, it's not clear how these polished philosophies relate to a job, yet one senses they are important. This ambiguity can cause a lot of stress for anyone needing to resolve the conflict between innovation and restrictive policy.

FIVE PITFALLS TO PHILOSOPHIZING

How much damage can corporate philosophies cause? Here are some of the drawbacks:

1. Ambiguous philosophies are hard to apply.

2. They are often created by a small group of employees and enforced on others.

3. Many employees resent being told what to believe.

4. Philosophy is theory. Business is a day-to-day hands-on activity.

5. Employees capable of "making things happen" may not be an integral part of the philosophy.

Mission, vision and value statements are extremely important to engage your workforce in a common purpose. **Companies whose employees understand the mission and goals enjoy 29% greater return than other firms** (*Watson Wyatt Work Study*).

U.S. workers want their work to make a difference, but **75% do not think their company's mission statement represents the way they do business** (*Workplace 2000 Employee Insight Survey*). In many cases, the fault lies not so much with the corporate philosophy itself, but in its application. Because employees are at the forefront of business activity, they first need to fully understand the philosophy so as to be in the position of applying it to various situations. Employees engaged in the development of the philosophy do not have difficulty in its application.

SIX STEPS TO ENGAGE EMPLOYEES IN YOUR ORGANIZATION'S PHILOSOPHY

Employees Before Philosophy

Which team is preferable?

1. A group made up of strong purposeful individuals?
   or
2. A strong purposeful group whose members think alike?

Strong purposeful individuals who think on their feet and define their own standards obviously make the better team. Most successful organizations have mission statements; most individuals do not. Like organizations, employees need a purpose for their work, a guiding mission that provides meaning to daily activities. Therefore, before engaging employees in a corporate philosophy, help them to first uncover their own sense of purpose in their work. The following example will illustrate why this is important.

When I was a retail manager, most of our staff was young and flippant about the job. This nonchalant attitude permeated the workplace; it was interesting to watch how quickly new staff adopted it as a means of "fitting in." Many defiantly proclaimed, "This job sucks!" and assumed an air of indifference. Workplace attitude defined their expectations of the job. Think of any new job you have had. When you first started, weren't you looking for signs that indicated the culture? How many infractions to the rules were tolerated? How far were employees able to push the limits? How much control did the manager really have?

STEP ONE:
Employees Need to Define Themselves
Outside of Others' Expectations

Corporate culture defines expectations that affect performance. This is why we need to help employees to identify and strengthen their own sense of purpose before selling them corporate expectations. If they wish to enhance their sense of purpose and ambition, employees must define themselves outside of the expectations of others. They must personally discover what is purposeful about the work, what they enjoy, and what success looks like to them. Employees with a strong sense of purpose are more accountable, self-motivated and initiating.

Strategy for "Individual Purpose"

To motivate employees into thinking about why they chose this line of work, pose this question: *Why are you in this job?*

The answers will vary. (The following are real answers drawn from a seminar.)

- The paycheck.

- I love my clients.

- There wasn't anything else.

- To support my lifestyle.

- It's a stepping-stone to something else.

- Social interaction.

- I have a great boss.

These are all good reasons and likely an employee's immediate response. Yet, if individuals search further, the answers will start to reflect deeper purpose.

Ask this next question: *What do you care about in terms of what you **do** in your job?*

Eventually the answers will sound more like this:

- Caring for and nurturing my patients.

- Helping clients feel good about themselves.

- Seeing the look of satisfaction in a customer's eyes.

- Helping patients be more responsible for their health.

- Knowing the product is making a difference.

- Being in a strong and sound organization.

- Knowing that the company values are consistent with my own.

- Honesty and integrity of business conduct.

STEP TWO:
From Individual Needs to Collective Purpose

Notice the variation between the answers in the two groups. As employees are asked what they care about in their jobs, the answers move away from individual concerns toward helping others, and building collective purpose. Employees must take care of individual needs before they can spare enough energy to contribute to others. Through coaching and follow-up, managers can help employees care for their own needs so they can free up their energy for the group good. As Maslow's *Hierarchy of Needs* teaches, humans need to satisfy lower-order needs such as food and shelter (wages) and social needs (interaction) before higher order needs, including purposeful work, will prevail. Maslow tells us that we are most motivated by our strongest needs. Management would do well to discover those personal needs among their employees and to motivate them accordingly.

The more employees reflect on the **joys** that called them to their work, the more their work becomes purposeful. If you join a financial planning firm and your manager tells you, "Your purpose is to help clients achieve financial independence," it isn't as meaningful as discovering a purpose for yourself. The good manager continually draws input from staff. Just as employees draw salaries, management needs to draw from its talent base. Creating conversations about things that matter to employees will at the same time generate for them a sense of identity. When employees have their own sense of purpose, they are not so easily influenced by the environment or the employees around them. They have defined a purpose for themselves that not even a change in management, a change in the job or other employees' negative opinions can take away.

STEP THREE:
Set Individual Standards of Excellence

In this step, coach employees to create standards of excellence that reinforce what is meaningful about the work for them. These are standards in the intangible areas of the work.

Ask your staff: What are your standards for . . .

- Dealing with difficult clients when they have been mistreated?

- Working on a multidisciplinary team?

- Coping with and embracing new change or technology?

- Working long shifts?

(Add other similar questions of your choice.)

At first, most employees will give you a blank look or create some very fantasy-like response. Let them know these standards are created for their own good and not simply to sound impressive. These are standards chosen to reinforce the personal meaning and **joy** of their jobs.

Example: A nurse is a strong advocate of effective patient education. This was one of the reasons she chose the nursing profession in the first place. Accordingly, her standard of excellence might sound like this: "I am committed to educating patients about the necessity and benefits of their medication and how it affects their well-being now and in the future."

When this nurse dispenses medication, it is a purposeful activity. She won't just say to a patient, "Open your mouth and swallow!" Her standards are clear and meaningful. They have an impact on her job performance.

How to Create Standards of Excellence:

1. Have employees set standards that reflect the joys that called them to their work.

2. Define standards and then ask employees what successfully implemented standards would look like (e.g. the highest quality service—What does this look like?).

3. Prompt a human response of standards of excellence. How does the client feel? How do employees feel? What actions specifically create these feelings?

Ask employees what success looks like to them. They will likely define success with words such as goals, achievements, confidence, overall comfort and skill level, attitude and specific abilities. Next, have them think about how they can immediately incorporate these values into their jobs. If employees were really "successful" on the job, then what would be different? Make sure employees understand how their strengths and skills add to the group's collective purpose. Strong habits succeed and prevail if you focus on them.

STEP FOUR:
The Mission Statement

Do you recall the movie *Jerry McGuire?* Tom Cruise's character lost his job because he risked voicing "the things we think but don't say"in the office. Jerry's concern was that the company had learned not to care enough about the business and their clients. Office apathy did mean something to Jerry McGuire. He declares he is prepared to die for "something" and "live for its cause."

The organization's mission is a unifying source that bonds employees and departments. Once employees are encouraged and aware of their individual purpose, get them focusing on organizational and group purpose. What is the purpose of their collective efforts? Mission statements and pat purpose statements don't work. A mission statement that isn't realistic can do more harm than good to employees and customers. Because it is false, it creates distance. For purpose to really work, we have to involve employees in it.

Let's say a delivery company's corporate mission is to be the "leading delivery company in North America with a solid commitment to deliver merchandise to its customers within 24 hours, in excellent shape and in a careful and courteous manner."

If it's clear and understandable, let's assume it's achievable. How do you make it real? Involve staff in the creation of the purpose statement. In many large organizations this is just not practical. Yet employees still need a say in the purpose of their activities. Here's how you involve them in the organization's purpose.

As a Group:

A. Break down the organization's mission statement into its separate aspects and,

B. Understand why each part is important to:

- the overall organization

- its clients

- immediate co-workers, and

- the individual job(s) in their department.

C. Apply it to the job.

Based on the delivery company's corporate mission statement described above, here are some expected answers to section A:

A. Break down the mission into its separate aspects.

   1. get merchandise to the customer

   2. within 24 hours

   3. in excellent shape

   4. in a courteous and careful delivery manner

Start with number one, "get merchandise to the customer," and discuss why this is important to your department or unit (if this is applicable). Of course, you want to discuss other departments as well, especially the departments most affected by your activities (e.g. the sales department is definitely affected by manufacturing). Go through all the departments and make an extensive list, and then go back to number two and start over again.

Broader Perspective

As your plane leaves the runway, objects on the ground become smaller as you distance yourself from them. Soon you see people as tiny dots on the pavement, then you see the entire neighborhood, then the whole city. As you step back from a situation at work, your perspective also changes. The further you remove yourself from the immediate concerns, the easier it is to achieve objectivity about your job, your co-workers' jobs and ultimately, the purpose of the whole organization.

Help employees become more aware of how their jobs affect the company as a whole. Ask staff to enlarge their perspective past the day-to-day operations. They will learn to focus not just on the short-term daily activities, but also recognize the link their jobs have to the bigger picture. Employees are more accountable and committed when they understand how others depend on them.

STEP FIVE:
Focus on Acceptance, Not Implementation

Focus on employees and their acceptance and understanding of the principle, not on implementation. Keep surveillance to a minimum; leave the implementation to them. Get individual employees to commit (based on what they care about and what they are good at) to keeping purpose alive. If you recall the movie Castaway, you will remember that the character played by Tom Hanks had an obsession with getting packages to customers within 24 hours. Even being stranded on a desert island didn't deter him from his need to "deliver the goods." It took him five years to do so, but eventually he got off the island and delivered that parcel to its rightful owner.

Surely someone in your organization shares a similar yet not so obsessive concern for delivery. Get this person to commit to making sure deadlines are met. Have that individual report back to the group with data, success stories, areas for improvement, etc. Of course, be sure you have a strong communication commitment through regular meetings, celebrations, newsletters and group projects. Break out of constricted job functions and break into employees' hearts and minds by involving their input and acceptance.

Entice Talent

Make sure managers know the strengths of individuals on their team by keeping a skills inventory, then summoning those skills to the project. Too often employees suppress their talents because the job doesn't provide an outlet in which to use them. If employees aren't using their skills and talents regularly, they may quit and take those talents elsewhere.

STEP SIX:
The Test

Every employee in the business should be able to answer the question, "What does your organization do?" Their answers should reflect the client's needs.

Ask fifteen employees at various levels of your organization to state the organization's mission. Record their responses; if they don't reflect the mission statement, it needs to be reworked and simplified.

Even more important is employees' understanding and acceptance of the mission. Go through the steps above again until you engage employees enough that they understand and accept the corporate mission. In this way you create a corporate culture that revolves around employees and their collective purpose.

Values Crumble
Making an Organization's Values Valuable to Others

The new employee walks into a meeting five minutes late. She immediately feels the need to justify her tardiness. She reaches across the table to choose a cookie and notices two managers shoot disapproving looks at each other and shake their heads. The new employee assumes this means, "Here is another bad apple." As the training continues, she senses pressure to ask clever questions to show she is keen and observant. She feels a sense of competition with the other new recruits. Each person is trying to outdo the next with a more impressive question or position. Meanwhile, the topic on the table is corporate values. The training manager hands out colorful values statement summaries that sets out how the company promotes a strong coherent team environment, trust and honesty between employees, and an empowered workforce. The keen new recruits all look to the management, smile sweetly and nod their heads as if to say, "Count me in on this team." This is a pivotal and unfortunate moment.

While all of the values suggested are very worthwhile, it's hard to convince others of the sincerity of your beliefs when you don't model it yourself. The organization promotes a strong team environment and yet management puts staff in the pressure cooker and steams competition amongst them. As the temperature rises, management and senior employees seem to say, "We are watching you" or "You may not fit into the culture here." The values statement summaries look good on paper but in reality, they're not happening. Employees are asked to promote values that, at some level, they question whether they really exist and thereby dissociate themselves. On the surface, some of these values may seem so basic that they insult one's intelligence. "Who says I'm not a team player?!" Slowly, the spirit crumbles.

Values: An Icy Sell

How do you sell attitudes, beliefs and values to employees? You can't; they have their own. You can teach employees skills, but you can't teach them attitudes. Hire employees who already believe in the same philosophies, and then engage and involve them.

FIVE STEPS TO APPLYING VALUES STATEMENTS

Employees naturally take on the values they believe and are engaged in. Instead of forcing values and corporate philosophies on them, get employees to buy in by involving them.

Take the following steps to involve employees in organizational values:

1. Make sure employees understand why the values are important to different departments, the company as a whole, suppliers, customers, and co-workers.

2. Get employee input. What do the values mean to them, why are they important and what do they really believe in?

3. Clearly define your terms. What is teamwork?

Who comprises the team? Am I in a team with the president of the company although I have never met that person? Which activities require teamwork and what would true teamwork look like? If you want to espouse a value, then explain what it is and show a clear example of it in action.

4. Create a task force to help implement, recognize and communicate values to others. The task force would be made up of the employees who really believe in the values to begin with.

5. Policies should support values and purpose statements, not contradict or ignore them. Never ask an employee to model something that is contradicted in some way by a policy or rule.

It Is Easier to Control with Policy Than to Create with Values

If your organization says trust is an important value, then why do you have such strict policies around employee sick days and miscellaneous budgets? If your organization says customer service is an important value, then why are returns such a hassle? If your organization says empowerment is an important value, then why do employees have to ask before making even the most trivial decisions?

Values are as important as policies but too often policies contradict values. Policies, which often limit a person's activities, are easier to create and implement than values.

When something goes wrong, we create a policy to prevent another occurrence—after the fact. Values and purpose statements, on the other hand, are developed to prevent erroneous assumptions from the beginning. Creating a workforce that is empowered and self-starting may mean creating something that isn't there already. It is easier to stop an incident from happening by controlling and regulating it (with a policy) than it is to create a values system (values like teamwork, service, trust, etc). But this is taking the easy way out. These are the intangibles that organizations need to survive in the future, so create!

MAKING VALUES REAL

1. Clearly define the value and give examples of it in action.

2. Solicit employees' input and definition of the value in their life.

3. Have discussions about why this value is important to the workplace.

4. Empower individual staff members to make sure values stay alive in the work.

5. Make sure policies don't contradict values.

A QUIZ: Organizational Philosophy in Action

Philosophy or Value:

_____

_____

Specifically, someone performing with this philosophy/value in mind would function like this:

_____

_____

_____

_____

I can clearly define this philosophy/value in action.

☐ YES   ☐ NO

Why we have this philosophy/value:

_____

_____

_____

_____

Whom it affects and how (customers, co-workers, suppliers, etc.) List them all:

_____

_____

_____

_____

Philosophy/ Values Implementation:

_____ % of our staff could answer the above questions knowledgeably. We have taken the time to train and follow up with employees about philosophies.

☐ YES   ☐ NO

Employees would say our philosophies and values are clear and understandable.

☐ YES   ☐ NO

If a policy contradicts a value or philosophy, employees have the discretion to overturn the policy.

☐ YES   ☐ NO

Managers model our values. (See them doing it before you say yes.)

☐ YES   ☐ NO

If you answered no to two or more questions, go through the exercises in this chapter again. If you are fuzzy about any of the answers to these questions, you need to redefine the ambiguous philosophy or value involved.

Keep the Focus on Employees

To keep the focus on employees, continually ask the questions that involve and engage them. "What was the best thing you learned this week?" or "What was the most difficult decision you had to make at work this week?" This personal introspection ignites a sense of involvement and commitment and makes the job more challenging and fun. But don't just ask the questions; listen, empathize, share them with others and challenge employees to do something with the information. Remember the answers and ask them again. See if the answers change. If not, why not?

Success Looks Like This!

Some habits die fast; others linger forever. They may endure because we are not aware of their patterns. Knowing is half the battle, so begin to squash bad habits by becoming aware of them. What if employees found out their habits were contributing to failure by damaging outcomes and destroying otherwise promising results? Managers can support employee growth by helping them become aware of the habits that bring about fruitless results. One warning: Don't have employees focus on weaknesses. Keep their attention on the success they want to enjoy.

ACTION PLAN

1. Activate the six steps to engage employees in your organization's philosophies.

2. Set individual standards of excellence.

3. Test your organization's mission statement.

4. Do the five steps to make organizational values real.

Chapter Eleven

Dealing with Cranky Co-workers and Clients

How to Banish Negativity to Keep the Joy of Work Alive

- Learn How to Stay Calm and In Control In Conflict
- Learn Four Steps to Deal with Negative Behavior
- Practice Handling Conflict With Ease and Confidence

Let's face it; some people's mood swings can gnaw at your sanity. Crankiness is infectious. It can spread through an office as silently and pervasively as a virus. You will do anything to escape the cranky person's subtle harassment and frequent emotional outbursts. Another's foul moods can become your liability, draining the **joy** out of *your* job. These unhappy individuals can deteriorate group morale, lower productivity, and scare away clients.

MIRROR, MIRROR, ON THE WALL, WHO'S THE CRANKIEST OF THEM ALL?

Unbelievably, most prickly people have no idea of their toxic attitudes. As psychologists suggest, knowing is half the battle because you can't change what you don't know and you can't see. How do you help cranky people to 'fess up to their mood swings? Can you hold up a mirror so they can see the villain

151

inside? Read on to find out how to "de-crank" the cranky. Before getting overwhelmed by their energy sapping demands, remember you are in control.

Sticks and Stones May Break My Bones, But Names Will Never Hurt Me

Remember that nobody can ruin your day until you give him or her permission. Only you ultimately control the way you respond to situations and people. This is very powerful. The next time someone loses it and tries to take it out on you, before you get upset or take on the blame, be assured that you have a choice. Do I let this upset me or not? Most things don't warrant your attention. If you work with someone who habitually flies off the handle, you will have to learn not to take it personally.

TIPS TO DIFFUSE CONFLICT:

- Diffuse hostility by relating to the other's point of view.
- Anger is not productive and the sooner you can calm the culprit down the better. Use statements like, "I can appreciate what you're saying" or "I've felt that way too" or "That's what I've thought for awhile" or "While that may be true..." Once you've calmed the other person down you can discuss things on a more reasonable level. If you can win them over, they will start to see you as an ally and trust in your opinion. This is where you have the power to influence their future behavior.

- Stay calm. Going straight for the throat is the worst thing you can do because people tend to mimic your behavior. If you get angry, they get angrier and you have just helped to fuel their behavior. When under fire in such a situation, use deep breathing, positive affirmations (e.g. "I will remain calm, "or" I can handle this"), or focus on the resolution.

- Back out gracefully. We are all human. If someone is on the attack and you're not in the mood to defend yourself, try diffusing the attacker and back out gracefully. "I can see you are upset, and we need to discuss this, but now is not the time. Let's talk about it later." It is far better to come back to that person after time out when you are both in the mood to discuss the situation.

- Use good body language. In situations of conflict, body language betrays your frustration and anger. Indicate you are listening by making eye contact, nodding, smiling, leaning forward, and paraphrasing what you hear.

- Verbally move the "complaint" along. Some people need to complain, so let them. Most people will get it out and move on. Others may see this as an opportunity to drag someone else through the mud. The best way to stop the complaints is to move it along. "OK, yes, alright... I hear you..." Once you get the gist of the argument, quickly reiterate their concern and move onto the solution. You don't have to be a victim of others' complaining, so instead of visualizing duct tape over their mouths, try paying attention and move the conversation along towards a resolution.

- Listen for words and emotions. When people are emotionally charged, they color their words with their attitudes. It is important to stay focused. What are they getting at and what does this mean to you? It helps to be straightforward and ask, "What are you trying to tell me?" Try to understand their basic needs and respond to them. Your responses may not solve their deeper life issues but they will set a positive tone in your relationship.

- Be solutions-oriented and not problem focused. Behavior that gets recognized gets repeated, good or bad. If you spend too much time wallowing in the problem it may just grow. Understand and sum up the problem and immediately focus on the solution.

- Use the "How can I help?" approach. "You seemed annoyed and withdrawn at the meeting when we really needed your input. What's wrong? How can I help?" Most frustrated employees really want to talk about the situation so they can move on.

- Never blame. When someone is upset, placing the blame back on him or her is dangerous. They are not in a position to recognize their faults. Avoid phrases such as: "You should have, you didn't, you can't..." These accusatory statements will only put others on the defensive.

FOUR STEPS TO DEAL WITH NEGATIVE BEHAVIOR

1. **Diffuse** the anger by relating to the problem. "I notice you seemed irritated by my patient and I can understand. Sometimes she is hard to deal with."

2. **Talk** about what you saw. "I saw you get really upset with Ms. Jones because she wouldn't take her medication."

3. **Ask** for what you want. "The next time this happens, can you just politely explain why the medication is important and assist her in taking it?"

4. **Wait** for agreement.

Sit down if possible when delivering criticism. Arguments tend to escalate when people are standing.

Crush Criticism

Squawking sour criticism behind co-workers' backs is destructive. Eventually, people become wise to cruel intentions and this begs for retribution. Stop criticism before it gets out of hand. Encourage employees to keep a positive tone when talking with co-workers. If they carry a grudge it should be dealt directly with the person they hold the grudge against. Be on the watch for criticism seeping into conversation and encourage critical colleagues to explore their feelings and come to terms with them.

EXERCISE: PRACTICE CONFIDENTLY CROSSING CRITICISM

Who are the difficult people in your life? Make a list of some who you have encountered in the last couple weeks. Briefly recall the situations. What did they say and how did you handle it? Now visualize it happening differently. What would you say that would calm the person down? How would you move the conversation along and resolve the issue? See yourself doing this in a very relaxed, confident and focused manner, positively affecting the relationship in the future. I suggest you do this visualization exercise once a week if possible. Then when you are in a tumultuous situation, all you have to do is call up this vision you have rehearsed in your mind and it will give you the confidence to handle the situation.

DISARMED BY HONESTY

Imagine this. A frustrated employee tries to provoke a co-worker. It works; he's mad. But instead of traditionally flaring up, he stops and realizes he's angry, reflects on the reason and responds with an honest expression of his emotion. He says, "I want to understand what you're saying and I'm feeling frustrated that we can't come to terms with this. I don't dislike your idea; I'm just finding it hard to concentrate because we are both so emotionally charged." There is nothing more disarming than an honest and clear expression of emotion. Honesty disarms crankiness.

If we don't deal with emotionally charged situations right away then we might carry emotional baggage that colors our relationships in the future. Be faithful to who you are and what you are there to do. Resist the temptation to let others derail your efforts.

ACTION PLAN

1. Practice the techniques to keep calm and in control in conflict. Write down the techniques that work best for you so that you can use them again.

2. Practice the four steps to deal with negative behavior.

3. Do the practice visualization—handling conflict with ease and confidence.

About the Author

As a professional speaker and writer, Jody Urquhart is committed to helping organizations be a more joyful place to work. Recognized in Canada, the United States and Europe, she has presented her signature topic, *Joy of Work*, for over 10 years.

Annually she addresses over 40 organizations and associations, and is a top motivational keynote speaker.

Jody's monthly column *The Joy of Work* is syndicated in over forty magazines and trade journals.

Jody is a feature speaker for the *GE Healthcare Tip-TV* program broadcast in over 2600 healthcare facilities.

Jody is the 2008 Bronze Winner of the 29th Annual *Telly Awards* for excellence in programming this presentation.

Jody holds diplomas in Professional Speaking from Mount Royal College and in Management and Marketing from the Southern Alberta Institute of Technology. She studied management for three years at the University of Calgary. Her business experience includes management positions in the banking, health care and retail industries.

Jody's clients include health care associations, financial, corporations, parks and recreation bodies, government departments and many more groups.

Jody was on the founding board of the Canadian Association of Professional Speakers, Calgary chapter.

To inquire about having Jody speak at your next meeting please call **1-877-750-1900**.

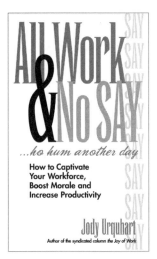

Do you like what you've read? Why not give *All Work & No Say* to employees, customers, colleagues or associates?

BULK DISCOUNTS AVAILABLE.

Please call us toll-free at 1-877-750-1900

Contact us via our website, or get our mailing address at

www.idoinspire.com

Please rush me _____ copies of *All Work & No Say*
@ $20 US or $20 CDN   = $ _____

Postage & Handling _____ Items @ $7.00/item (US or CDN)   = $ _____

7% G.S.T. for Canadian orders   = $ _____

TOTAL — please check either ☐ CDN $ or ☐ US $ = $ _____

Ship to (Name): _____

Organization: _____

Address: _____

City _____ State / Province: _____

Country: _____ Zip / P.C.: _____

Phone: _____ Fax: _____

Email: _____

Method of Payment:

☐ Check—**Please make payable to Jody Urquhart and send to the address on our website**

☐ Online—**Please refer to our website for online payment details www.idoinspire.com**